The SOSTAC® Guide
To Your Perfect Digital Marketin

C000257687

by PR Smith

Voted in the Top 3 Marketing Models worldwide by the *Chartered Institute of Marketing's Centenary Poll*, the SOSTAC® framework can be learned in 3 minutes. That's why more and more professionals use it across the world.

"Highly acclaimed planning system – even for experienced digital marketers." David Green, Head of Global Digital Marketing, KPMG

*"Although most businesses are now doing digital marketing, nearly half don't have a plan – that's shocking! SOSTAC® gives you an **awesomely simple framework** to put that right."* Dave Chaffey, CEO Smart Insights

V6.2 Feb 2020

Contents

Acknowledgements

Many thanks to Hugo Rubio for really pushing me to write the original SOSTAC® Guide. I have been asked many times to do it by other people but Hugo was the most persuasive. He flew over from Bilbao, sat down and talked me through the reasons why I should write this. Hugo has also helped me to improve the content in many different ways. Un saludo Hugo.

My thanks to Dave Chaffey (Smart Insights) with whom I have co-authored Digital Marketing Excellence. Dave & I discuss SOSTAC® intensely regularly and Dave's feedback has been invaluable. Thanks to Davy McDonald (book cover) and Brian O'Neill (website) with whom I work closely on many digital marketing projects around the world. Thanks also to Mike Hollingsworth for the internal graphics. In summary, thanks to:

Alex Adamo, Adamo Enterprises
Dr. Anthony Buckley, Technological University Dublin
Beverly Barker, Course Leader IDM
Mike Berry, Course Leader IDM
Ged Carroll, Marketing Strategist & Planner
Dr. Dave Chaffey, CEO Smart Insights
Osama Fawsi, Business Development Manager, ITV Agency
Andy Fernandez, Bookshop & Library Manager CIM
Alex Gibson, Host, The Persuaders
David Green, Head of Global Digital Marketing, KPMG
Mike Hollingsworth, Graphic & Web Design
John Horsley, Chairman, Digital Doughnut
Dr. Etain Kidney, Technological University Dublin
Jez Lysaght, Marketing Consultant
Bernard Marr, CEO, The Advanced Performance Institute

Ian Maynard, MD, Ian Maynard Marketing
Mike O'Brien, CEO, Jam Partnership
Paul O'Sullivan, former Dean, Technological University Dublin
Michael Ranasinghe, co-founder Sri Lanka Golf Tours and cofounder Synergy School of Marketing
Tim Redgate, Personalisation & Content Consultant
Charles Randall, Head of Solutions Marketing, SAS
Michael Rogers, KPMG Management Consultant
Hugo Rubio, IBM, Spain
Ahmed Sabry, CEO Digital Marketing Arts Academy
Mohamed Sameh, Digital Mktg Manager, ITV Agency
Ben Salmon, Marketing Data Technologist
Richard Sedley, CEO EY-Seren & Partner EY
Adam Sharp, MD, Clever-Touch.com
Adam Smith, Marketing Manager, Zenith Optimedia
Cian Smith, Creative Content (SOSTAC® Memes)
Jay Thorogood-Cooper, CEO Bloom Worldwide
Lawrence Tracey, Principal, Wolf Networks Inc.
Tom Trainor, CEO, the Marketing Institute of Ireland
Jon Twomey, MD, Student Support Group
Colm Williamson, editor, WaterfordWhispersNews.com
Ze Zook, co-author, Marketing Communications

Thanks also to the ever patient and lovely Beverley, who put up with me locking myself in my study for months so that I could produce this, SOSTAC® Guide to Writing the Perfect Digital Marketing Plan.

About The Author

Paul runs workshops, advises and mentors as well as writes books about digital marketing. Someone once told him that there were 17,000 Paul Smiths in the UK alone, so with his initial being 'R', he adopted PR Smith as his pen name.

Paul enjoys engaging audiences in workshops & conferences

Workshops and Talks

Paul's workshops, webinars and conference talks have been described as 'inspirational, innovative, insightful' and are always delivered in a carefully structured manner so that key points are easily remembered and, more importantly, actioned. Although intense sessions, delegates have fun too. prsmith.org/training

Adviser/Mentor
Paul has helped to boost the results of, literally, hundreds of organizations from blue chips to innovative SMEs, whether mentoring, consulting or on an advisory board. Recent projects include creating 'golf on paradise island' – the 'Pearl in the Indian Ocean' (Sri Lanka Golf Tours) and a 50 year project connecting Northern European wind-farms with Southern European solar parks via SuperNode.Energy to deliver all of Europe's energy requirements. prsmith.org/consulting

Author
His seven books are published in seven languages. America's Jim Sterne refers to Digital Marketing Excellence as 'a must read'. The CIM refer to Marketing Communications as a 'Marketing Major', while SOSTAC® Planning in various books, is voted in the top 3 marketing models worldwide. prsmith.org/books

Academia
Paul is a visiting lecturer at the Cass Business School (London), the Institute of Direct and Digital Marketing, the Marketing Institute of Ireland, the Dublin Institute of Technology and he speaks in Europe, the Middle East and the Far East. He is a Fellow of the Institute of Direct and Digital Marketing and a member of the Chartered Institute of Public Relations, with a BSc Management from Dublin University, a PG Dip Finance from Southbank University and an MBA from Cass Business School.

Other Publications by PR Smith

Smith, PR and Zook, Z. (2020) Marketing Communications
– integrating online and offline, customer engagement and
digital technologies, 7th ed., Kogan Page
Chaffey, D. & Smith, PR (2017) Digital Marketing
Excellence – planning & optimizing your digital marketing,
5th ed., Routledge
Smith, PR (2011) SOSTAC® Guide To Writing Your
Perfect Plan, prsmith.org available on Amazon
Smith, PR (2003) Great Answers To Tough Marketing
Questions 2nd ed, Kogan Page
Smith, PR, Berry, C. & Pulford, A (2002) Strategic
Marketing Communications, Kogan Page

Business Blog prsmith.org/blog
Sportsmanship Blog www.GreatSportsmanship.org

Interests
Paul is 35 years happily married to Beverley, whom he
says, "is the most patient wife in the world". They have
three, now adult, children. Paul enjoys reading, music,
sport and travel, plays football, touch rugby and golf.

Paul is also author of Great Moments Of Sportsmanship (book) and founder of the (Not-For-Profit) Great Sportsmanship Programme designed to inspire youths through inspirational short stories about sportsmanship.

So, if you think the world now needs more integrity, respect, friendship, honour and nobility, please join me in our social- media- driven campaign  to change the world, bit by bit, by inspiring youths, schools, colleges, universities, clubs and whole communities into sportsmanship values.

The Programme comprises story-telling sessions and an educational programme (teaching pack: workbook, slides, the book and online resources/stories, videos and posters). Boosting literacy, self-esteem and global citizenship.

All based on true, two-minute stories that inspire young people. Students love it.

Whether reading stories or watching videos for fun or as part of a short educational programme, in schools and clubs, this programme changes behaviour and attitudes. Watch the 4 min summary video on the home page of GreatSportsmanship.org and/or the 14 minute TEDx Talk Paul gave called 'How Sportsmanship Can Save The World'. Or Google 'PR Smith TED', or go to youtube & search using 'PR Smith Sportsmanship'.

To select stories from either a particular sport or a specific country Scroll down the right-hand side of www.GreatSportsmanship.org Join us as an ambassador and mobilise a new generation of global citizens. Introduce us to a school or a club, or alternatively, just, sit back and enjoy the stories.

Great Sportsmanship.org

Great Sportsmanship Programme

Great Sportsmanship

GtSportsmanship

Great Sportsmanship Programme

Great.sportsmanship

SOSTAC® Feedback

All feedback is most welcome via the <u>form</u> on my website <u>prsmith.org/feedback</u>.

Allow me to apologize, in advance, for any inconsistencies in the layout and style of this self- publishing format. Your patience is much appreciated. Please do send feedback.

Thank you to those of you who sent me interesting content. Most of the content, links, videos, articles and tweets that people send me are shared on my various social media platforms (see below).

I particularly seek examples of creative marketing, that delivers great results. Ideally, driven by analytics or market research.

You can get updates, discuss posts and tweets or contact me about advising, coaching or speaking at your next event via any of the platforms listed below.

PRSmith.org

PR Smith

PRSmithMarketing

PR_Smith

PR Smith Marketing

PRPSmith

SOSTAC.org

Preface

Although this is a quick guide to writing the perfect digital marketing plan, it has taken many years to write it as a short guide. I have used SOSTAC® in all of my marketing plans and clients love it. I also use it in all of my text books in various editions over the years including:

Digital Marketing Excellence – planning and optimizing your digital marketing

Marketing Communications – offline and online integration, engagement and analytics

Why use SOSTAC®?

SOSTAC® is
- simple
- clear
- logical
- memorable
- structure

It can be used as a template that ensures consistency when presenting plans from different teams, departments or regional offices throughout an organization, whether local, national or global.

People like SOSTAC® as it clarifies and simplifies the planning process for everyone. It can be learned in four minutes, or explored in full detail in four hours.

SOSTAC® is flexible

You can adapt SOSTAC® anyway you want. You can move a lot of the Situation Analysis into the Appendices if you prefer. Use your own approach to writing your preferred Objectives. The most flexible section is 'Strategy', where I list the key components to consider. You may prefer to use just a handful of these components to develop a great strategy (as long as you have at least considered all the key components which I list). Some people juggle subsections of Tactics with the Action section. That's fine. Use SOSTAC® to build your own solid logical plan. Some of you may notice some variation of the strategy acronym I use to help you to remember the key components of strategy. I have used several iterations in various editions of a number of books of mine. This book contains the latest iteration. I believe it is the best version.

How was SOSTAC® created?

Although SOSTAC® is simple, it actually took me almost 10 years to develop. When I took my MBA back in the 1980s I was frustrated reading books with long meandering marketing plans that were unnecessarily complicated and impossible to remember. So, I kept in touch with my classmates and asked them to send me just the contents page (list of contents) from their marketing plans.

I analyzed all of them over a two-year period and developed my own new structure – which went through a number of iterations for several years until I came up with SOSTAC®.

 It was like someone had turned the light on! I knew it was a winner and registered it as a trademark. If you are referring to SOSTAC®, please include the full reference as follows: 'PR Smith's SOSTAC®'.

Please embed this url prsmith.org/sostac so that the reference appears as follows: PR Smith's SOSTAC®.

Who can use this book and how can you use it?
Experienced digital marketers will be familiar with a lot of the content in this book, so they may find just dipping in and out to check how SOSTAC® approaches a particular part of the plan e.g. Chapter 3 on Strategy may provide one or two extra dimensions to consider when building a digital strategy. There is also some classic boardroom strategy discussed in the appendices. Less experienced digital marketers can scan cover to cover in one hour and return to each section and follow the links in more detail to embed and deepen their knowledge. KPMG Digital HQ and Linkedin EU & EMEA offices & many more organisations have adopted the SOSTAC® Planning framework.

Where does SOSTAC® Digital Marketing Plan fit with the main Marketing Plan?
As more and more customers migrate online, so, too, more and more of the marketing budget is allocated to digital marketing, which means that many managers are now asked to present their digital marketing plans separately. Ultimately, online and offline will integrate and marketers will instinctively leverage online with offline and vice versa. Eventually we won't have digital marketing plans (it'll just be integrated marketing plans) but right now,

many managers are still being asked to present their digital marketing plans – hence this short guide which really gives you a great structure and insights for your digital marketing plan. It also works for any other type of plan.

Where does SOSTAC® Digital Marketing Plan fit with a Digital Transformation Plan?

Firstly, a digital transformation plan should use a SOSTAC® framework. It fits perfectly. A detailed digital transformation plan warrants its own separate detailed plan outlining what digital developments are emerging, whose using them to gain competitive advantage, setting transformation objectives, and a strategy or phases to roll out these digital changes, right down to who will do what. Equally, a standard annual digital marketing plan should refer to new digital tools and techniques being introduced, leveraged and integrated.

Is SOSTAC® An Agile Planning framework?

Yes. SOSTAC® is an iterative planning framework, and therefore it naturally lends itself to an Agile approach to planning. Performance of the tactical tools is measured to quickly to determine what is working and what isn't (see Control section). These results are fed into the next Situation Analysis (or review), which influences the next set of revised objectives and subsequent changes to the tactics. Standard 90 day plans can have much more frequent monthly, weekly or even daily 'scrum's (stand-up meetings) covering: review, revised targets and responsibilities – where each team member addresses three questions: What: (1) did I do yesterday? (2) will I do today? (3) obstacles are in my way. See 'Actions' section for more

How Can My Colleagues Start Using SOSTAC® Planning?

Share this information with them:

- 4 min SOSTAC® summary video & infographics
  SOSTAC.org

- 60 min Udemy online course
  Udemy.com/_sostac_plan/

- 20 hours SOSTAC® Certified Planner online course
  SOSTAC.org

- 1 & 2 day SOSTAC® Masterclass workshops
  prsmith.org/Training

- Licensed SOSTAC® templates to help you quickly
  write your own plan (in both word and powerpoint)
  prsmith.org/Contact

Introduction to SOSTAC®

So here it is: SOSTAC® + 3Ms in one minute.

Situation Analysis – where are we now?
Objectives – where do we want to get to?
Strategy – how do we get there?
Tactics – the details of strategy (the marketing mix)
Actions – ensuring the strategy & tactics are executed with
            excellence and passion (internal marketing)
Control – measurement and metrics to see if 'we are getting
there or not'.

+ 3Ms (the three key resources):
Men and Women (human resources);
Money (budgets);
Minutes (time scales)

And now, if you want, you can see this on video, in a bit
more detail, in four minutes via the website
prsmith.org/SOSTAC, or watch it later and continue with
the book.

Visit prsmith.org/SOSTAC
watch the 4 minute video.

SOSTAC® is a registered trade mark of www.PRSmith.org

PR Smith's SOSTAC® Plan

Chapter 1 Situation Analysis

SOSTAC® is a registered trade mark of www.PRSmith.org

Situation Analysis Is Critical to Future Success

Arguably, the greatest marketing book ever was written
over 2,000 years ago. The Chinese military strategist Sun
Tzu wrote The Art of War (translated version Wing, 1989).
Most senior marketers have a copy of it on their shelves. It
has become a classic read, particularly for some
enlightened marketing managers. Interestingly,
confrontation, or war, is seen as a last resort and the best
military strategies win the war without any bloodshed.
They win wars through intelligence.

Sun Tzu effectively confirms why the Situation Analysis
needs to be comprehensive.
Here's an excerpt:

Those who triumph,
Compute at their headquarters
a great number of factors
prior to a challenge.

Those who are defeated,
compute at their headquarters
a small number of factors
prior to a challenge.

Much computation brings triumph.
Little computation brings defeat.
How much more so with no computation at all.

By observing only this,
I can see triumph or defeat.

'Much Computation' or much analysis is required. The better the analysis, the easier the decisions will be later. Decisions about strategy and tactics become a lot easier when you know your customers, your competitors, your competencies and resources as well as market trends.

That's why **half your plan should be devoted to the Situation Analysis**. It doesn't have to be at the front of the plan (you can dump a lot of it in the appendices) but the detailed analysis must be carried out if you are to succeed.

Hence almost half of this guide is devoted to the Situation Analysis. The first year you do this analysis, it will be particularly challenging, but as you find better (and often free) resources for highly relevant information, this analysis gets easier, the intelligent information gets stronger and, consequently, you make better informed decisions. This ultimately boosts your results.

More good news – there is a plethora of new listening tools available to marketers. Although traditional market research is still useful, there are faster ways of monitoring online discussions and analyzing customers, competitors and spotting trends.

We will explore these.

'All markets are conversations'
declared the influential Clue Train Manifesto (Levine et al, 2000). The subsequent rampant growth of social media since that time confirms the validity of this now classic digital book.

The Old Marketing Ship Is Sinking
All marketers need to monitor, analyze and engage in these conversations since the old 'shouting' model (advertising and PR) is no longer as effective as it once was.

Today's marketing models involve careful listening to customers (and prospects) online (as well as offline) and giving fast responses to changing moods, needs, issues and trends that are occurring online continually. Marketers don't have a choice. This is not a luxury set of tools. These new listening tools are 'must haves'. See <u>Social Listening Skills</u> for more information on each of the tools discussed on the next few pages.

Other tech developments such as AI (Artificial Intelligence), VR (Virtual Reality), MA (Marketing Automation), IoT (Internet of Things) and Big Data must also be embraced (more on these later).

The Old Marketing Ship Is Sinking
Photo courtesy of DavyMac.com

What Should the Situation Analysis Contain?
Your Situation Analysis should be so thorough that it makes your decisions almost risk-free.

Your Situation Analysis should contain a thorough analysis of:

1.1 Customers
1.2 Competitors
1.3 Partners (and intermediaries)
1.4 Competencies (including Strengths and Weaknesses)
1.5 Performance/Results
1.6 Market Trends (including Opportunities and Threats)

1.1 Customer Analysis

Your Customer Analysis needs to be so thorough that it ensures you know your customers better than they know themselves.

If you could only ask three questions about your customers (& your prospects), what would you ask?
Remember, you have limited resources, the 3Ms: Men (and Women), Money and Minutes. A limited number of people (men and women) who can help you find this information. Limited budget (money) to hire people, commission market research or buy reports. Limited time (minutes) to search, find, collect and digest the information. So, you have to choose your questions carefully.

How To Make Better Decisions

Before making any major decision, ask yourself:
'Do I have all the information I need to make a great decision?' In other words, what questions do I need to ask before I make a great decision?

What would you ask?
Try these three big customer questions:

Who?
Why?
How?

You'll find that most questions about customers will fall into these three categories. So if you can master these questions, I mean, get detailed answers, then you'll find choosing which channels and which marketing tactics becomes a lot easier, and your marketing results will, ultimately, improve.

'Who' usually gets the weakest answer

Who exactly is my ideal customer or visitor (or prospect or decision maker)? This is often unclear or even undefined when making marketing decisions. What kind of traffic do you want to attract? What is the profile of existing customers? How can you find your ideal customer if you don't know who they are? It's like 'looking for a needle in a haystack' except you don't know what the needle looks like! So you have got little or no chance of finding it unless you spend an unnecessary large amount of resources. This is 'hit-and-miss' marketing, or worse still, 'hit and hope' marketing. We'll look at defining segments and using personas to precisely answer this question in more detail later in this section.

'Why' is the most difficult of all three questions

Because customers often don't know and don't tell you 'why' they buy or don't buy, or why they register or don't register, or why they follow, like, share, visit, stay, bounce (leave quickly) or return to your site. Many customers themselves don't even know why they buy. There are often unconscious reasons driving their behaviour. Ask people why they drink Coke or why they 'Like' Coke's Facebook page and they almost always give rational reasons when, in fact, it's for mostly emotional reasons (I know you probably disagree – now do you get my point?).

'How' do customers buy?
Includes, 'What is their digital journey?' or if you prefer, what is their 'multichannel path to purchase?' What route do they take (via search engines, PPC ads, website, referral site or any other mix)? How many visits? When do they search for information, when do they decide and when do they buy? All of these questions generate answers to another question: 'When is the best time to post content?' How do customers change channels, say, between reading offline media and interacting with online media and then visiting a physical location? Equally, 'What are my competitor's prices?' might be categorized under 'How' much do my competitors' customers pay?

Become customer obsessed and master the 'Who, Why and How' questions.

You can categorize questions whatever way you prefer, but either way, Who, Why and How, may help you to categorize and remember at least these three big questions. It may help you to remember many of the other sub-questions which you also want to ask about your customers.

Master these questions and you are taking your first step towards being a world class marketer. Put it another way, without in-depth answers to these three key customer questions you are playing a dangerous guessing game, while your competitors may be discovering and using valuable customer insights to gain competitive advantage via understanding (then serving and nurturing stronger relations simply because they know your customers better than you do). Make your organization 'customer obsessed'.

Now let's look at each of these in more detail and start with the question that many marketers cannot answer: 'Who is your ideal customer?'

**Most Marketers Don't Know
Who Their Customers Are**

Only 45% of marketers are capturing and consolidating customer behavioural data from multiple channels in a single database (Forrester, 2013). That was then. Do you know the profile of your ideal target customer/s?

1.1.1 Who?

Defining who is your ideal customer makes it a lot easier to find new customers and to decide which types of customers are worth spending resources on. In summary, Customer Profiling helps prospecting, winning and retaining profitable customers.

Who is that ideal customer who will be pleased to hear from you (as opposed to feeling disturbed by your intrusion and therefore not having the time nor interest in your special message)? What is the 'ideal customer' profile? Can you clearly define them? Who are your Facebook visitors, your LinkedIn visitors, your YouTube viewers, your Instagram sharers and your website visitors?

Did you know that each of these platforms provides tools giving you insight on your visitors? For example:

- Facebook Audience Insights
- YouTube Analytics
- Google Analytics demographics

Are You Searching For (an invisible) Needle in A Hay Stack?

If you can't define exactly who is your ideal customer, how can you ever find them? It's like looking for a needle in a haystack, except you don't know what you are looking for since you don't have a clear customer description or profile.

Not knowing your customers is like looking for a needle with a blindfold on!

Don't become another fool in the dark, continually searching for customers without being really sure who you are looking for nor what is their profile.

Why wear a blindfold when doing marketing?

**Knowing your ideal customer
- makes finding new customers easier**

Once you have clearly defined the profile(s) of your ideal customer(s), it now becomes easier to find similar 'ideal customers'. Without a clear definition you are looking for a needle in a haystack (and you don't know what the needle looks like!) A well-defined customer profile, stops all the aimless searching. Combining some of the new targeting tools and new databases, with clearly defined 'ideal customer' profiles saves you time and money and boosts results when we look at targeting in the Tactics section.

In addition to the old B2C demographics (job, age, gender, location, income etc.) we can now add psychographics (interests, attitudes and personality attributes) as well as technographics (their technical and online click behaviour can reveal their needs and more). Where and when do they go online? On which device(s)? What kind of content do they engage with? What do they share?

Business to business (B2B) segmentation variables typically include: industry sector, job type, size of company, location, centralized or decentralized, benefits sought and even attitude to risk. Today we can add many new variables like interests (pages viewed), topics discussed and more. Depending on the number of market sectors you operate in, you may have more than one type of 'ideal customer'. More on this later.

So, let's start with some classic 'Who' questions:

- Who is your ideal customer?
- Who are your visitors and what stage of the buying process are they at?
- Who are your followers?
- Who are your influential customers, visitors and followers?
- Who else is talking about your type of product (and what are they saying)?
- Who is attending a particular conference or event (and what are they saying)?

- Ask your data and you shall receive (answers)

Who is your ideal customer?

Having converted a percentage of your visitors to customers and entered them onto your database, the next question is: Who are your best customers? Which ones are more likely to respond to your offers? Which ones should you target with special offers? For many decades now, database marketers have used RFM (Recency, Frequency, Monetary) to help to identify those active customers that are more likely to continue buying throughout their customer lifetime. See Tactics for more on RFM.

Isn't this a shame?

'I've spent most of my life not knowing who the customer is. Isn't that a shame?' Lyor Cohen director at Island Def Jam & Warner Music Group. (Sisario, 2014)

Personas

Personas bring target segments to life by describing, in more detail, the different types of customers that exist within a segment. As well as the usual demographics, personas include favourite media, type of car, partner's job type and interests, webographics (web experience, usage, location, platform) plus a statement related to the product such as: 'I've got loads of ideas and enthusiasm, I just don't know where to start.' Three or four personas are usually enough. The primary persona should be an important customer for the business plus 'needy' from a design point of view (e.g. 'technically challenged' or a 'beginner user'). Personas have been used in advertising for decades.

Today's digital marketers use personas to focus on delivering the right content and overall online experience.

Personas

A thumbnail summary of the characteristics, needs, motivations and environment of your typical types of visitors, prospects and customers.

Here is a heuristic persona template from Steve Jackson's, Cult of Analytics (2011). It basically covers:

- Tasks prior to purchase
- Considerations and questions
- Pain points
- Search terms
- Key paths/content

Goals	Insert Goal - Determine your persona's key motivation or reason for visiting your website. Note that it's the persona's goal not necessarily your business goal. This data about key motivations comes from the research stage.
Scenario	Describe the persona's typical scenario and reasoning for visiting your site. What would be the typical way that the persona would know about your product or service? How would they find out about the product or service? What specific methods are involved in reaching you? How would the person do his/her research?

Tasks prior to purchase	Tasks prior to taking action – Determine all the tasks the persona will need to accomplish before being in a position to take the action you want them to take. What does he/she need to find out? What is his/her first major concern about the product or service? What are the next 4 factors that need to be understood in order to have a better idea of all the risks involved?
Consid- erations and questions	Considerations From the scenario and the task list determine what questions your persona may have about your product or service. It should be relatively easy at this point to come up with around 10 key questions that the persona would want answered before deciding to purchase.
Pain points	Pain points Will be different for each persona and very personal. What makes the persona cry out in frustration? If he/she is potentially defecting from one product or service to yours, what pains him about the current situation? If not, what are the needs that really pain him/her the most?
Search terms	Based on the pain points and considerations Trigger terms are words people look for or use to try and solve their problems. Used in search engines, on blog posts, in emails. Determine 5 terms that will be used to search on search engines that relate to the pain points and

	problem the persona has. It's good to do prior research around these keywords on Google Keyword tools.
Key paths/ content	Determine the paths that the user has to take to answer all of the questions/considerations and solve all the pain points the user has.

You can see a completed persona for a young man called Tapio in plus a variation which includes customer journey in Appendix 1.

It is good practice to develop several different personas for each particular target market.

Personas are important. They help copy writers to ensure your website, content marketing, ads etc. are written to help specific people in real, specific situations.

> Copy that is written for the average prospect.......
> is written for no one in particular
> and often fails miserably.
> Use personas to tighten up your copy writing.

Scenario Planning
Scenario planning identifies different scenarios that personas may have while using the product or service.

While Personas describe typical users (and their needs, goals, and motivations), Scenario Planning describes the actual usage (or event/s) while using that product, service or website. There may be several scenarios, as in the case of a chocolate company's website which might have visitors who want chocolates for a wedding, other visitors want to express their love and others may want the chocolates for a dinner party (3 different scenarios).

You can see, arguably, the best ever example of scenario planning, by National Semiconductor (who makes B2B chips for mobiles) in Appendix 2. Their scenario planning used just one scenario to cover design engineers and in doing so, they boosted enquiries, sales, repeat customers, lifetime customers and actually created sustainable competitive advantage.

Jobs to Be Done
Today, Chris Christensen's term, JTBD, reveals how customers visit a web site to complete a particular task yet many of them struggle to complete the task (or 'job to be done'). JTBD shows how companies can help them better – particularly digital services. More later.

Who are your visitors?
You can see your visitor profiles from your analytics package. This information is automatically collected (and freely available from Google Analytics). This tells you what percentage of your visitors come from which locations and via which devices. Google Analytics now also guesstimates the gender and age of your visitors. Google also reveals, in aggregate, what these visitors are interested in (see 'Why' later). Similarly, Facebook Insights gives aggregate data on age, gender, location and interests of your visitors/fans as well as which content generates most engagement.

What are their interests and stage in the buying process?

Although this question helps to build a profile (describing who your visitors are), it also overlaps with the 'Why' question as their click behaviour (what they click on and the 'duration' or length of time they spend on it) leaves a trail of their interests, what engaged them and what didn't. Click behaviour is also called 'digital body language'. Either way, an individual's interest and stage in the buying process can be recorded (see KPMG example, Appendix 3) and also, the aggregate behaviour can be recorded i.e. how many visitors were interested in certain products or pages. Some data service companies offer to layer on an individual's interests which are taken from publicly available social media 'interests' declared.

Customer Journey Mapping
These maps, or illustrations or diagrams show the details of all of your organisation's touchpoints that your customers come into contact with as they try to get a specific 'Job to Be Done' completed plus the emotions they experience during that journey.

You can see Neil Davey's (2018) 9 different customer journey maps (and what we can learn from them) in this link https://tinyurl.com/ybf3d2g5

Identifying what buying stage a visitor is at via Key Phrases
Keywords used in a search engine can indicate how advanced a potential customer is in their online buying journey. People searching with specific key phrases self-categorize themselves into a particular stage of the buying process.

For example, searchers using the following key phrases:

- 'electric adjustable beds' could still be in the research phase
- 'electric adjustable beds reviews' – getting close to being ready to buy.
- 'buy electric adjustable beds' - likely looking to make a purchase soon.

You can find actual terms and volumes using Google's Keyword Planner. You do have to set up with Google AdWords, but use of the tool is free. It's essential if you're interested in learning more about your customers.

Here are some simple stages customers go through

1. Research Phase
It's worth remembering that your potential customer may only be aware of their pain, not the solution. However, focusing on prospects who seek a solution and are in the initial research phase of their buying journey, the initial keywords they start searching with might include: Electric adjustable bed, electric adjustable bed tips, electric adjustable bed help, electric adjustable bed advice, best electric adjustable bed, cheap electric adjustable beds.

2. Advanced Phase
These prospects have done some research. They know what they want, and now need to create a 'considered set' of just a few brands that they like. They may also be interested in finding the best quality for the least money. At this point, they are looking for reviews and comparison shopping. Keywords or phrases indicating this stage of the buying journey might be:
'electric adjustable bed reviews'
'compare [your brand name] with [your competitor brand name]'

3. Buy Phase

At the final stages of a sometimes, tortuous journey, these buyers are very focused and ready to buy. They'll be using these kinds of phrases:
'buy electric adjustable bed'
'purchase electric adjustable bed'
'get electric adjustable bed'
'electric adjustable bed signup'
'contact electric adjustable bed'

They want an easy, convenient, clearly sign-posted route to buy (with options – some want to buy over the phone, others in person and others prefer the website.) Therefore, they need easy to find information, contact details, phone numbers, references and proof of quality.

**Want to get potential customers
from your competitor?**

Try '[Keyword] coupon' in a Pay Per Click ad. Generally, people search for this term when they're ready to buy. Offer your lead a discount that's automatically added to their cart/signup (and make the checkout process simple), so they go through you and not the competition. (Tiffany da Silva, 2014)

Now have a look at how KPMG, one of the world's top four professional services firms identify 'Who Is Their B2B Visitor' (and the visitor's possible needs from their click behaviour). They categorize/segment visitors into 'Visit Type' according to their click behaviour which is based on 'how the visit originates, how it ends and/or what happened during the visit'.

15 Categories (or segments) KPMG Use
to classify who each visitor is according to their on-site behaviour (i.e. their click behaviour, or their digital body language):

1. Prospect (submits a Request For a Proposal [RFP] or an email to a partner)
2. Participant (registers for an event, the site or content)
3. Passive Browser (downloads single articles, papers, starts but doesn't finish a video)
4. Researcher (downloads multiple articles, papers, starts and completes more than one video in multiple practice areas or industries)
5. Advocate (reads an article or paper, or views a video and shares it)
6. Focused Seeker (reads multiple content items within a practice area or industry)
7. Passive Job Seeker (reads content on the Jobs Section of the site)
8. Engaged Job Seeker (submits a job search query and views job details)
9. Participating Job Seeker (submits their résumé)
10. Brand Aware Visitor – First Time and Repeat (a visitor that comes to the site directly)
11. Responder (responds to a KPMG email campaign, or clicks on a link within an alert or newsletter)
12. Brand Aware Searcher (comes to KPMG website through branded SEO, PPC, display ads on third party sites)
13. Non-Brand Aware Searcher (comes to KPMG website through non-branded SEO or PPC)
14. Passive Social Visitor (comes from a social media property (Facebook, Twitter, YouTube) one time)
15. Engaged Social Visitor (comes from a social media property (Facebook, Twitter, YouTube) and

conducts one of the Engagement actions described in the Metrics Taxonomy)

You can see a more detailed table in Appendix 3.

What are their names, jobs and addresses – using registration data?

You can, of course, ask your visitors to register and tell you who they are, and in return you can give them some content that is relevant to their needs. People will not give up personal information unless there is a personal benefit to them.

Remember you can only collect limited individual profile information and names via registration. I say 'limited' as it's best not to ask for too much information too early as it annoys customers and reduces conversion rates.

How HSBC conversion rates increased by 2,000%

by reducing the number of questions from 17 to 4 questions. See the Actions section for more.

What are their names, addresses and interests – using reverse forensics?

Some visitor analysis use 'reverse forensics' to identify approximately 20% of the visitors to a B2B website by identifying the visitor's IP address, url, company name, location, general contact details (including general telephone number), what page(s) each visitor was interested in (and duration), what phrases they used when searching and now you can pair that data up with other services to find actual people in specific job titles (telephone number, email address and social information).

Additional customer information from progressive profiling

You can continually add information about customers and prospects from, firstly, each interaction on the website, and secondly, from different sources both online and offline.

If you have an integrated database and the automated processes, you can continually upload relevant information to ultimately build a better visitor profile. So, each click on a website combined with public profile information on various social platforms, layered with other public databases can build an even more detailed profile of your customers.

> 'Tying customer behavioural data
> from all online and offline sources with
> past purchase and customer service history
> to segment and communicate with the buyer
> in a personalized fashion
> previously only dreamed of.' (Eloqua, 2013)

Who are your followers?

Who are your Twitter followers?

You can see where your Twitter followers come from and how influential they are (Who) and when they go online (How) by using Followerwonk.com (or similar services).

Who is your Facebook audience?
Facebook Insights gives free analytics which reveal the
demographic breakdown of your fans/followers/audience
and also which time and type of content generates more
engagement.

Who are your LinkedIn followers?
LinkedIn Company Page gives you free Follower Analytics
which reveals followers' demographics and sources, which
content gets read and how you compare to competition (see
the 1 min. video called 'Get Insights with Company Page
Analytics'.

**Who are your influential customers and
visitors/followers?**
Who are the influencers that spread your content? How
many do they reach? What content was received well?

Knowing who's interested in what you have to say helps
you to get to know them and ensures they always see your
content. Here are some services that identify your
influencers and what interests them:

- Crowdbooster.com identifies who is influential that
  shares your content.
- BuzzSumo identifies influencers (it also identifies
  content that's performing really well under different
  keywords and phrases).
- Followerwonk identifies location, language, gender
  and influence of your Twitter followers and also
  helps measure yourself against competitors' audit
  and track followers.
- Google's Referral Analysis (Google Analytics)
  shows you who is linking to you and referring
  traffic to you and which referral sources get you the
  most traffic and are the most influential.

Other service companies identify any influencers automatically once you insert a key phrase, brand or company; they identify who is talking about it and, most importantly, who are the most influential ones.

Some influencers are AI driven avatars like Lil Miquela (see prsmith.org/blog) and others, like Shudu (the world's first digital supermodel), is the brainchild of of a young British fashion photographer who self taught himself 3D Modelling via youtube videos. Like other models, Shudu influences people. Unlike other models Shudu is an avatar created by Cameron-James Wilson.

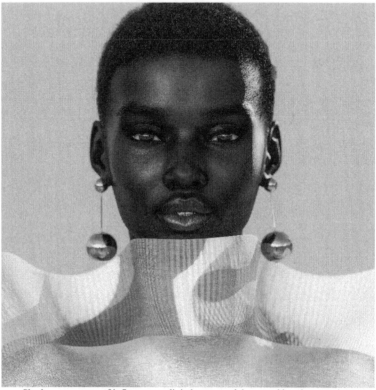

Shudu, a new type of influencer, a digital supermodel, created by photographer, Cameron-James Wilson

Back to B2B markets, new services can also find who are your Influencers according to their level of influence, segmenting based on location, industry, company name, conversations, hashtags or any other business field e.g. Find me: 'influential twitter users, who are based in London and who work at companies in the finance industry where their revenue is greater than £200 million per year'.

'There's too much talking in social media
and not enough listening and learning.' (Brian Solis, 2012)

---

7 Ways to see who is talking about your product (or your type of product)?
taken from The Old Marketing Ship Is Sinking on prsmith.org/blog:

1. Listen to customer service

2. Listen to customer feedback:
   Reevoo, Feefo and Trust Pilot

3. Listen to customer communities:
   GetSatisfaction, UserVoice and UserEcho

4. Listen to local chatter (Twitter), Twitter Search's 'advanced search' (see box) and listening to Mentions and Messages on Twitter via TweetDeck, Hootsuite, SocialBro TweetReach, Tweriod and Twilert.

5. Listen to multiple websites (feed readers).

You customers are talking about you
Photo courtesy of hubspot

6. Listen to influencers: Followerwonk identifies your influencers' demographics location, language, and gender of your Twitter followers. It also helps track your followers and measure yourself against competitors. Google Alerts (now called GigaAlert) and TalkWalker, _ and Mention.com are worth considering.

7. Listen to the mood of the market – Sentiment Analysis. Social Mention (blogs, comments, bookmarks, events, news, videos), TwitterSearch: search by topic, people, hashtags, words, exact phrase, 'near this place', BoardReader (forums and boards), Google Blog Search, WhosTalkin.com (mostly free).

There are some paid-for tools that summarize all the conversations and deliver a single sentiment score as well as allowing you to drill down and engage in those -

conversations, namely Radian6, Alterian (now called SM2), SysomosMAP and Brandwatch.

See Who Is Talking About Your Product Type via Twitter's Advanced Search

Using Twitter's standard search engine you can find people talking about a certain topic (#topic), companies, brands or people or even tweets from particular people.

You can narrow your search to a specific region or to people who are looking for your product (brand or general category) in a specific area, or who are talking about a competitor. <u>Twitter Advanced Search</u> can do this for you and a lot more.

See the 'Actions' section for more.

Who is attending a conference or event?

We can generate databases of people who attend a particular conference or event, what they say about certain topics and contact details, once they tweet comments with the conference/event hashtag. See the 'Tactics' chapter for more on this.

Your customers are talking about you – but are you listening?

Photo courtesy: Hubspot and PR Smith

Ask your data and you shall receive

Data can be integrated analyzed and used in so many new ways. Your ability to ask good questions, may determine your future success. See how you can search data for new customer profiles in the Tactics section.

**Your Facebook 'likes' reveal your
sexuality, race, drug use & your parents' divorce**

Individuals can be analyzed on Facebook to reveal a lot more about an individual. For example, new analytics software from Microsoft and Cambridge University (tested on 58,000 volunteers) analyses and identifies a person's private and very sensitive personal attributes based on their Facebook 'Likes' such as your sexual orientation, drug use, religious and political views, intelligence, happiness, age, gender and more. Could your 'likes' be analyzed before a job interview or a major negotiation? (Cambridge University and Microsoft, 2013) See how Cambridge Analytica used facebook data to 'swing' major political campaigns in prsmith.org/blog

---

Your Tweets' linguistic footprint reveals your real personality

IBM's Twitter psycholinguistics (analysis of anyone's choice of words when using Twitter) can 'reveal an individual's personality traits from just 200 of your tweets in 20 seconds' (Takahashi, 2013).

Extracting correlations between a person's word choice (and activity patterns) can reveal these intrinsic traits as dutiful, conscientious, conservative, introvert.

These 'linguistic footprints' (in the public domain) can now replace (or enhance) the old segmentation variables. They can also identify if you are happy or depressed (different words used).

How Did Trump Win?   Precise Targeting Helps

A small English company who had also worked on the Brexit 'Leave' campaign for UKIP, worked for Trump and divided the US population into 32 personality types, and focused on just 17 states. Obviously, there's a lot more to it than just that (we'll reveal more later in this book) – but being clear about the first level of 'Who?' is invaluable in any campaign. Smith, PR (2017). See also 'How Trump Won' on prsmith.org/blog.

See an organization's previous websites
'The Wayback Machine' (now called the 'Internet Archive') reveals all previous versions of a website which, in turn, reveals how a company is changing (e.g. mission statements, Unique Selling Points, Online Value Propositions, size of team/staff, old product ranges and more). Useful when doing a sales pitch, or proposing a strategic alliance or even before a job interview.

Who else is in a client's staff?
LinkedIn Advanced Search lets you insert a company name to see how many people work there (or in a particular department), how many are in your network, or you can search by location or industry type.

If you are in B2B, you can even learn about prospective customers with company size (employees). Although 'advance search' tab does not appear, most of the functionality is still there when you search for a company or industry sector, a company or a person and then the search filters appear on the right hand side.

Linkedin Sales Navigator has additional new features regarding prospects such as their interest groups, any articles or comments posted, any conferences recently attended and any time a prospect is in the news.

Once you know the 'ideal customer' profile, you can then find new customers

The Tactics chapter will briefly explore how new databases, new ad networks, and new targeting tools can be exploited, once you know who is your ideal customer.

For now, let's move onto the second big customer question: 'Why?'
Why do some visitors not convert to customers?
Why do my customers buy from me instead of competitors?
Why do visitors visit my site?) .... read on!

1.1.2 Why?

Why do customers buy or not buy from you? Why do they visit or not visit your site? Why do they come back a second time to your site? Why do other visitors leave or 'bounce' after less than 30 seconds? 'Why' is the most difficult of the 'Who, Why and How' questions. Sometimes this is because customers themselves, don't fully know why they buy.

The good news is that, in addition to the traditional offline market research techniques, there is a plethora of new online tools (many of them are free) which help to answer this, sometimes complex, 'Why' question.

Without knowing the answer to the 'why' question, marketers waste resources by offering the wrong proposition. For example, the multi-billion dollar football industry, doesn't know why their customers (fans) buy their services. Many football businesses will not survive; in fact, many football clubs in the UK are losing money constantly – despite receiving huge TV & sponsorship revenues and having amazing customer loyalty levels (with lifetime value multiplied by share-of-wallet) that most marketers can only dream about.

Most marketers don't fully know what their visitors' interests are

Only 45% of marketers are capturing and consolidating customer behavioural data from multiple channels in a single database. (Silverpop/Forrester, 2013)

Has this improved since then? Do you know your visitors?

There is a great online opportunity to get customer insights that were never previously available freely and quickly. Many businesses combine offline focus groups and surveys with online insights (discussions, analytics and surveys). These customer insights can be fascinating – whoever imagined that customers would have a 'relationship with a tin of paint'........

A relationship with a tin of paint

People walk in and choose Dulux paint. They don't know why they choose Dulux paint. It might be to do with the shaggy dogs in the ads, but it is a sad fact there are human

> beings in our country who have a relationship with a tin of paint. (Laurie Young, 2014)

'Why?' is a difficult question,

e.g. why do football fans watch football?
A few years ago I asked some Manchester United football fans 'why do you buy tickets for the games?' They didn't actually know the real reason! So they couldn't tell me. None of them mentioned the word 'football' or even 'to see a football match'. It is extraordinary. It is also true. Watch the video.

See Man Utd. fans talk about why they buy
on YouTube: PRSmith (NB this channel only contains older video clips – for more recent clips visit youtube channel PR Smith Marketing

If using Maslow's Hierarchy of Needs, it seems that football satisfies middle level needs ('to be loved').
I wasn't happy with these answers, so I took a camera crew to Harvard Business School to interview the late, great Professor Ted Levitt.

He told me that fans going to football, or ice hockey, or a rock concert enjoyed 'a transcendental affair' (i.e. the highest level Maslow needs were being satisfied). Subtle stuff, but I am convinced that he was correct.

Many UK football clubs lose money – possibly because they don't fully understand why their customers buy, i.e. possibly they don't understand that they are selling a 'transcendental affair' to both the fans inside the ground and the millions around the globe who seek: 'unconscious relationships and transcendental experiences' via football?

AnswerThePublic.com
Enter a keyword, brand or phrase and this site generates questions that are asked about the keyword, brand or phrase

---

See the late, great, Professor Ted Levitt
on youtube

Finding the answer to why customers buy is not easy. Offline questions/discussions and even surveys often fail to extract the real reason. However online digital body language based on actual customer click behaviour (including what phrases they use to find the site) does not lie. Web analytics don't lie. Now let's explore the complex 'why' question.

Here are some 'Why' questions (which we will answer)

- What are your customers' needs? What do they really want?
- What do your customers like (or dislike) about your product/service?

- What are your customers' future needs?
- What are your online visitors' needs and what are they interested in (what is their 'job to be done'* when they visit your site or store)?
- Why do your visitors only return to some sites??
- Why do your visitors not convert?
- What marketing content do your visitors specifically like?
- What marketing content do influencers like?
- What part of your content (e.g. a webinar) does your audience like?
- Why do people tweet? Are they like rats? Read on.

*Clayton Christensen (2016) 'Job To be done'

How to Double Your Sales – by Asking 'Why?'

If 20% of your visitors move through your web site to the pricing page, yet only 2% convert into a sale, find out why 18% SCAR (Shopping Cart Abandonment Rate) via a pop-up survey. If you convert just 10% of this 18% that equals an extra 1.8% (call it 2%) of customers on top of the original 2% = 4% conversion. Congratulations, you have just doubled your sales!

What are your customer needs?
In addition to listening to customer service feedback (including customer text dialogue with your chatbots – they are already transcribed for you!!), use customer reviews and traditional offline market research to ask customers what they want and what their preferences are. You can also see customer needs expressed via the phrases they use in search engines (on your web site search engine).

This is valuable information as the web site's customers are succinctly describing their needs in their words (not yours). Once you understand customer needs you can then work backwards.

e.g. Specs for Amazon's big new projects, such as, its Kindle tablets and e-book readers are defined by customers' desires rather than engineers' tastes. 'If customers don't want something it's gone, even if that means breaking apart a once powerful department.' Rule no. 5 of Amazon boss, Jeff Bezos's 10 Leadership Lessons (Anders, 2012)

Airbnb was going bust until they asked 'who?' & 'why?'

In 2009 Airbnb had 20 customers per night and were going bust. Co founder, Brian Chesky was asked by an investor 'where do you get most traction?' he answered 'New York' to which the investor asked 'why are you here?' Chesky flew that night to NY and started visiting his customers' homes – to find out what they loved and what they didn't like. This identified customers' needs. From that they worked backwards.

'I don't feel comfortable with guests in my house.'

Asking customers their likes and dislikes revealed the following: 'I don't feel comfortable with guests in my house' to which Chesky replied: 'well, what if I did this?'….. 'What if we added in their profile?'

This is where the Handcafted CX is born. Chesky asked: 'What do you want in a profile?' Answer: a photo. 'What else?' Answer: Where they work? 'What else?' Answer:

> 'Where thy went to school?' 'What else?' Answer: 'How
> they behaved in their last Airbnb venue?
>
> The creation of the peer review system delivered even more
> reassurance with customer support from customers
> (Hoffman 2017)!

What are your visitor's needs and what are they interested in?

Identifying key phrases (used to search for your product or
service) and 'click behaviour' (number of pages, visits and
average duration) reveals what your visitors are interested
in.

Although Google has recently made it more difficult to see
these key phrases, you can link Google Search Console
with Google Analytics to identify key phrases (See
SmartInsights.com's Google Search Console and SEO
Effectiveness for more).

Ask visitors 'What did you come to our site today - to do
what?' via an on-site survey.

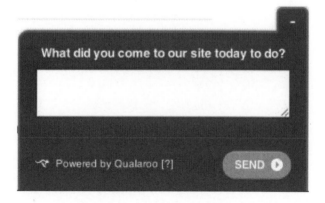

A short (3 questions) on-site exit pop-up survey

1. Why did you come to this site today? [dropdown list of possible reasons]
2. Did you achieve this [ ] Yes No [ ]
3. How else can we help you? [open text answer]

As Christensen (2016) says – 'what is your job/s to be done?' or as McGovern (2017) says 'What is your task/s to be completed?' once you know these, you can then define what you need to provide customers to get the job done quickly and easily. Check is there anything that you are not providing them that you do?

Follow the conversations:
Get Alerts About What Customers/Markets Want
It's worth mentioning some of these tools again: GigaAlert (formerly Google Alert) for alerts about any topic by journalists and major bloggers; other agencies identify who is discussing what and how influential they are and where they are based; Followerwonk.com identifies who your Twitter followers (and influential followers) are; news readers like feedly.com monitor several blogs; Sentiment Analysis actually summarizes all conversations and puts a score on the sentiment or mood which reflects what's being said about a brand. It also allows you to drill down, see who is saying what and with the option of responding.

Why does your community exist?
If you have a community, you need to be crystal clear why it exists. Understanding why your community exists and why customers like your community is fundamental to your future growth.

You'll be pleasantly surprised to learn that it is not always about discounts.

Why Did Some People Vote For Trump & Brexit?

The worrying phrase 'post-truth' was even named Word Of The Year by Oxford Dictionaries (Flood 2016). Defined by the dictionary as an adjective "relating to or denoting circumstances in which objective facts are less influential in shaping public opinion than appeals to emotion and personal belief". PR Smith 2017

What do your customers like (or dislike) about your product/service?

Useful customer feedback comes from product review services like Reevoo, Feefo and Trust Pilot, who track down customers and get product reviews. Customer

Communities like:
- GetSatisfaction
- Uservoice
- UserEcho

discuss products and services and reveal what customers like and dislike. Some brands even own their own customer panels (see NASCAR example).

Biggest Sport Uses Fan Councils

The world's biggest spectator sport, NASCAR, combines online listening tools, including online official NASCAR Fan Council (customer panel) to gather information about what the fans like and don't like about the user experience online and offline.

As mentioned, Website Pop Up Surveys can ask a few short questions about what customers like or dislike and more general online discussions can be monitored for comments about, and mentions of, your products (and your competitors' products) via social listening tools already mentioned (and also discussed on prsmith.org/blog).

What are your customers' future needs?

Can you anticipate your customer's future needs? Yes, RFM, Customer Life Cycles, Collaborative Filtering, Time/Date/Event/Purchase triggers and social media Likes can all indicate a customer's likelihood of purchasing. Here's a brief description of each. See Tactics for more.

Future needs: RFM

A customer's Recency, Frequency and Monetary spending is a useful predictor of the probability of them continuing to purchase.

See Tactics for more.

Future needs: customer life cycle

Many companies measure a customer's LTV (Life Time Value) since if they deliver a great service, they can retain a customer for their buying life.

And it's possible to predict when they are ready to purchase again. See Tactics for more.

Future needs: time triggered, date triggered, event triggered and purchase triggered

Time may trigger a purchase such as six months after a car is bought it needs its first service. Date triggered events like birthdays or Father's Day triggers more buying and purchase triggered means buying product A means you will also, probably need product B.

Future needs: collaborative filtering

Collaborative filtering makes intelligent guesses at what else a buyer might like to buy e.g. when you buy a book from Amazon they check to see what other books buyers of this publication have also bought. They then offer these highly relevant additional books to you.

Future needs: Facebook 'Likes' increase propensity to purchase

There is a logical correlation between 'liking' a brand on Facebook and an increased propensity to purchase.

So, a highly engaging Facebook activity could support an increase in sales.

See Tactics on whether to increase spending on Facebook.

Anticipating future demand for new music via deep twitter analysis

Music is the most popular topic on Twitter. Although there were 1B+ tweets about music last year, this gold mine of data has not yet been mined. Twitter data is much sought after – CNN are partnering with Twitter to develop a news alert for journalists. Music company, 300, is partnering to scan for excitement about new bands (particularly from influencers) and then get alerts. 300 now has access to Twitter's data pile, including information not in the public domain such as the location tags that identify from where a tweet was sent. "The goal, is to mine Twitter for the kind of signs that music scouts have always sought, like a flicker of excitement about a fledgling band" said Lyor Cohen. (Sisario, 2014).

Why do your visitors only return to some sites ?

Jacob Nielsen's original research into why visitors come back a second time revealed the same four key factors year after year. The percentages vary each year but the same four satisfaction factors pop up repeatedly:

1. Relevant Content*
2. Easy Navigation
3. Quick Download
4. Fresh Content
   * Watch out for the unbelievably relevant rewards given to customers in the TD Bank video in the Tactics section. This video makes many viewers cry.

Does your website satisfy your visitors?

Find out. Ask your visitors. You can use a short pop up satisfaction survey. Or at the very least, you must do some Usability Testing' to ensure your website is fully functional and easy to use. The Control section explores these in more detail.

Why do your visitors not convert?

Why do, say, only 2%, of your visitors convert (e.g. download a white paper, register for a newsletter or take a trial or buy)?

It could be a combination of attracting the wrong type of visitor or they are unable to convert because your site makes it too difficult for them. You can compare your conversion rate with others.

Also see the 'Control' chapter for more.

Incidentally, if you assign money values to goals (such as 'sign up for newsletter' is a prospect worth, say, $10 or 'fill in an enquiry form' is a qualified lead worth £50. Ecommerce tracking is set up, you can also see how each page assists in conversion (through the Google Analytics Page Value metric).

What marketing content do your visitor specifically like?

Analytics packages like Google Analytics reveal which products (specific pages) are most popular (number of visits and duration). Most analytics packages reveal which content gets the most engagement. Site customer feedback surveys also tell us more about visitor needs – particularly 'unmet needs' i.e. what else they'd like to see.

What marketing content do your influencers really like?

Referral data reveals which people, or sites, link to which pages on your site (i.e. which of your pages appeal to other website owners). This tells you firstly, who is linking to you and secondly, gives you some clues about what content to focus on creating.

Note: referral data is available through several sources, for example, Google Analytics or other analytics systems. Google Webmaster Tools shows you what specific content external sites (or bloggers or influencers) link to. You can also monitor which of your tweets get retweeted by influencers using, for example, Hootsuite.

Observe influencers

See what their most popular posts are. See what questions

they ask on different social platforms. Engage in their discussions. Eventually ask these influencers what content or topics they might like to see. Or perhaps, if they might like to see a sneak preview of certain content.

You can constantly improve by asking customers (and prospects) great questions -even granular ones such as 'which part of a webinar did you enjoy most?' You need to prioritize your questions and not ask customers for too much of their time.

What part of your content (e.g. a webinar) does your audience like?

You can ask your audiences to do a 1-minute post webinar survey to analyze what your visitors actually enjoyed about the webinar, such as the presenter, the presentation, the topic (i.e. 'why they liked it?') and if there are additional topics they'd like to know about.

Why do people share things?
We share things to build our own personal brand and look good online.

What is being said about you locally?
You can listen to conversations taking place near you (geographically e.g. within a 25km radius of where you are, or within a certain country).

Twithawk and Twitter Advanced Search can find people talking in real time about your chosen topic, listen to them and, if you choose, easily engage with your audience mid-conversation.

Most customers talk 'about you' rather than 'with you'

Only 9% of tweets mentioning companies start with @ which means 91% of people are talking about you, not to you. (Radcliff, 2014). Has it improved since then?

Why do people tweet? Are they like rats?

One interesting theory suggests that we behave like rats when we tweet. We quickly learn that the more polarised your opinion, the more followers you get. We learn how to grow our followers by being more extreme. It is a vicious circle that has serious implications for society. Today's angry, polarised tweeters get rewarded with more engagement, more likes/shares/followers the more polarised the opinion. So like Skinner's Rat experiment in the 1940s, we learn how to win rewards (more followers). See: How Rats Work = How Twitter Works? Smith 2019 prsmith.org/blog

Understanding customer needs in the future - emotion recognition

Future communications systems will detect a customer's mood and tailor responses accordingly.

AI will use 'Emotion Recognition' (detected by voice if using voice operated software or by your choice of words used in search engine or Tweet or a Facebook post).

Face recognition and good old body language recognition will follow

---

AI Facial Recognition
Recognises Truth and Happiness

Clysedale Bank in the UK is already using facial rec. to measure customer satisfaction as customer leave the bank. While an American insurance company invites customers to record themselves on video, via their mobile ('smart phone') to make an insurance claim. AI Facial Rec. of truth + previous history/past records determine payment within an hour.

(PR Smith 2017)

Essentially, 'context is king', hence tailored responses that are relevant to your mood, your company, your device, your location, and your past history will achieve better response levels.

Also recognizing a customer's device, location (and time of activity) reveals different types of needs a customer might have. Tailored responses will be more relevant and therefore get better responses.

Facebook can even predict when you are going to change a relationship

Recent attempts by Facebook's data science team shows the incredible power of analyzing data. For example, Facebook revealed that it can now safely predict when a user is about to change their relationship status from 'single' to 'in a relationship'.

The insights come from analyzing the way we exchange messages and post on our timeline just before we 'commit'. The question is, what else will Facebook be able to predict? (Marr 2014). Sophisticated predictive analytics teams have been around for years (Duhigg 2012).

Targeting Who and Why For Future Success

In the 2020 race, facebook could theoretically determine not only who are the 32,578 swing voters in Pennsylvania, but also what you need to tell each of them in order to swing them in your favour. ...The market is less likely to self-regulate the explosive powers of bio engineering and artificial intelligence. (Harari 2017)

What's trending?
Sites like Google Trends and Trendsmap.com (twitter) let you see what's trending in different places. Who is speaking and what is being spoken about in different regions around the world.

This can also be useful for small local business owners who may have a small, community-led audience, as it will allow them to identify the key topics in that local area and to weave these topics into their marketing efforts. Google Zeitgeist (previously known as the Zeitgeist report) reveals what captured the world's attention in the preceding year - our passions, interests and defining moments as seen through search. It is now summarized on video.

Trending: Rage - Were Voters Angry? Why?

What the elite missed was the sources of the anger & resentment that has lead to the populist upheavals in the US & Britain & many other parts of the world. (They) assumed it's anger against immigration and trade and at the heart of that is jobs.

But it's also about even bigger things, about the loss of community, disempowerment, & social esteem (a sense that the work that ordinary people do is no longer honoured & recognised (& rewarded).' (Sandel 2017) Did this apply to UK BREXIT vote also and the subsequent successful Conservative election win whose slogan was 'Get Brexit Done'?

One trend that we see is the merging of online and offline.

"The superficial line between the offline and the online will eventually disappear as wearable technology and connected smart devices become the norm" (Anders Sorman-Nilsson, 2014). As audio search or voice-controlled, intelligent personal assistants such as Siri, Alexa, Sophia, Watson, Fin and many others will leave us hands free – disengaged from technological devices and simply surrounded by people and space in which is inhabited by the omni presence of these immediate 'virtual' assistants.

So, it's not surprising that the 'Why?' question is the most difficult question to answer. It requires a deep understanding of your customer's psyche. Create a culture of customer obsession.

**Why do we do what we do -
What do people really want?**

Uniqueness - people want to feel unique.
Connectedness – yet people want to feel connected to others. Paradoxically, we also need to feel we belong, that we are not alone in the world and that we are part of something larger (Adams, 2014). We are complex. Understanding 'Why' we buy' can be difficult. Do you agree or disagree?

Some offline tools help us to gather some customer insights and many new online tools help us to find answers to the final question 'How? – how do customers buy?' Read on.....

1.1.3 How?
So we've looked at 'Who?' and 'Why', now consider 'How?'. By this, I mean two things: how do your customers actually buy (what are their processes/steps or journey), and how do they process information? How do customers make their decisions? How do they discover your site? By what route (or what was their digital journey)? Did they move between online and offline? Which particular digital channels get the best visitors (i.e. traffic that converts towards a goal)? Channels include

advertising (PPC and banner ads), social media, direct mail, referral links, (using your web url).

Here are some questions which analytics help to reveal customer insights:
- How do customers buy (what is their online journey)?
- How long and how many channels do your visitors use?
- What stage are your visitors at in the buying process?
- When is the best time to post content and engage?
- How do your customers process information?
- How do customers prefer to view initial information?
- How do customers perceive your website?
- How do some videos work better than others?
- How do some words work better than others?
- What percentage of your visitors view your site on a mobile?
- How do customers see things differently on their mobile?

How do customers buy? What is their buying journey?
Customers generally make more than one visit to a site before buying. Their multiple visits also often come from many different channels, whether a general organic search (via a search engine) or a branded search, a PPC ad, a link or by directly inserting the web address into a browser.

Just like in football it is often the last pass, or assist, that is as important as the scorer of the goal (or the last channel in this case).

So we need to know which route generates the most conversions (or sales). Google's Multi-Channel Funnel Analysis does this (you'll find several videos on YouTube). Analytics packages answer almost all of these questions. As long as you add some Google Analytics code to each page of your website and tag all your email and ad campaigns (add a tiny bit of code which can be automatically added by marketing services), then you can access all of these reports and see which routes (or customer journeys) deliver the best conversions (within the last 2 months).

Remember 'conversions' are predefined goals, such as moving a visitor onto a specific page; signing up for a newsletter; a free sample; a trial period, or even making a purchase. More on Google Analytics and tracking campaigns in SmartInsights.com.

You can even filter via campaign or keywords to see what's working by using Google Analytics Multi-Channel Funnel Analysis (Keyword Assisted - Assisted Conversions Report) so that you can invest more in what's working and stop what's not working. Continually analyzing these visitor journeys helps marketers to continually optimize their returns on investment.

How long and how many channels do your visitors use?
The Path Length Report reveals how long (in days and in interactions) it takes for visitors to become customers.

The Top Path Conversion Path Reports reveals the paths visitors took on their way to converting to a customer, the number of conversions from each path, and the value of those conversions. In other words, this in turn, reveals which channels generate (or even just assist) more conversions than others?

How Long Do Netflix Customers Spend Buying?

Great question. Answer: 90 seconds! After that they give up and look somewhere else for a film that really interests them.

Netflix discovered that if customers didn't find a movie they wanted to watch within 90 seconds – they gave up – Netflix lost the sale & the customer wandered over to a competitor's channel/platform. Netflix now use big data to understand what each customer really likes & suggest relevant films. This use of data has generated $1b extra sales.

Which channels do your customers use?
Social channel identification tools identify where your target audience are communicating about your brand, your competitors and other relevant topics, i.e. if most of your customers' discussions are on LinkedIn and not Twitter, you should invest more resource on LinkedIn groups, advertising etc. See Tactics for more.

Web Site or Chat Apps?
Companies see large clusters of customers preferring instagram, Facebook (falling) or Whatsapp rather than simply web pages

With 2.5 billion customers using instant messaging [IM] on facebook, Whatsapp and China's WeChat (Economist

2016) an opportunity opens. Within a couple of years IM will reach about half of humanity i.e. 3.6 billion, (The Economist 2016). Some of these chats and messages will be AI driven bots who can handle millions of comments/questions with personalised responses (see Instagram's Lil Miquela) prsmith.org

What stage are your visitors at in the buying process? As mentioned in the 'Who' questions, click behaviour leaves a trail of visitor interests - what they clicked on (what engaged them). This is digital body language.

It also reveals how advanced a visitor is in the buying process. Also as a rough rule of thumb the longer the typed-in search term indicates the further the customer is in the buying process/journey.

Voice Search
Gartner has previously predicted that in 2020, 30% of online searches will be made on devices without a screen i.e. by just speaking to a device. Personal Assistants such as Cortana from Microsoft , Alexa from Amazon Echo, Siri from Apple, Google Assistant and the Smart Speaker, Google Home as well as Alice from Yandex, AliGenie from Alibaba and China's iFlytek with its accuracy of 98%, compared to Google's 95% (Castleman 2020) will become more popular particularly when they connect via IoT into devices, clothes and other objects.

The Invisible Supermarket Shelf
Will Voice Search change how customers buy? Personal

assistants like Alexa help customers find answers, information and products by asking the device for help. Optimising for voice search is important as just one answer or suggestion may be served /delivered (instead of a Search Engine Results Page serving six or more suggestions on the first SERP). See Tactics for how to optimise for voice search.

When is the best time to post content and Engage?
As abhorrent as it may seem, not everyone is on Twitter 24/7. So it's best to tweet when they are firstly, online and secondly, on Twitter. Tweriod identifies the best times for you to tweet by analyzing both your tweets and your followers' tweets to help you tweet at the best time. Other analytical tools identify when is the best time to post on Facebook and other platforms.

When is the best time to send an email?
Email newsletter platforms like Mailchimp analyzed over one billion emails to discover that after 12pm and in particular between 2-5pm on Thursdays were, on average, the best time to send an email. Use analytics to determine when is the best time for your industry sector – this will increase your open rates and conversion rates. Some businesses now see success by tailoring their email 'send' time for each customer based on the time when visitors first or last interacted. Another American analysis from WebMarketingToday suggests Fridays, Saturdays and Sundays were best as busy people catch up with their emails over the weekend.

It really does depend on your industry as travel businesses often say Monday is the best day (when people need a lift!) You've simply got to test your emails in a disciplined way and you will learn exactly when is best to send and to post. Nearly all email platforms have their own customer insights or analytics which tell you, (amongst other really useful information) when is the best time to post content.

How do your customers process information?

We need to know how customers look at our website, our email shots, our ads etc. Do they see the key things we want them to see? How do they process information?
In small chunks, is the answer. Customers process small chunks of information initially.

How do customers prefer to view initial information?

We are drawn to visual media. We have less time, shorter attention spans and more distractions as we multitask.

**The shift towards visual and social
Picture paints 1000 words**

Blogs have 500-1000 (or more) words
Facebook has just a few words*
Twitter: 140 characters** YouTube: no words***
Vine: 6s video - ditto
Pinterest: no words
Instagram: ditto
*Facebook posts with pictures and videos get more engagement
** Tweets with pictures get more engagement
*** well, very few words – just some in the title, caption, credits and description (and the full transcript plus annotations can also now be included)

Adapted from Joe Dalton (2012)

See also 6 tips to exploit this visual opportunity in chapter 5, 'Actions'.

So, perception is a delicate and highly biased variable. Just because you have made the most beautiful website, Facebook page, Instagram photos, ad, email or virtual event, doesn't necessarily mean the customer will also see it as beautiful. Customers may not be able to see it, read it, click it or use it because they don't see what you want them to see. Therefore, we have to test everything.

Shrinking Attention Spans

The world's first televised presidential debate was between Nixon and Kennedy in 1960. Harvard University predicted that the average attention span was 42 seconds. Kennedy responded in 40 second site bites. JFK won.

In 2008 attention span had dropped to less than 12 seconds. 'Yes We Can' seemed to fit the time available! Obama also won the 2012 race (8 seconds). Then in 2016 (4 seconds) Trump won with a short snappy slogan: 'Make America Great Again' (and of course a hash tag #MAGA). What was Clinton's snappy slogan?

In the EU, the BREXIT campaign won with a short snappy slogan: 'Take Back Control'. What was the Remain Campaign slogan?

Neither Trump nor Brexit got into policy details. This fitted with shrinking attention spans. Think about why you like reading these vignettes?

You can see President Obama's head of digital, Teddy Goff, discussing with me how they used customer insights (particularly behavioural insights) and big data to deliver a winning 2012 campaign on my YouTube channel 'PR Smith Marketing' (NB the separate 'PR Smith' channel hosts my old video interviews with world gurus)'.

You can also see a detailed analysis of exactly how Trump shocked the world and won in 2016 with some cutting-edge marketing prsmith.org/blog 'How Trump Won'.

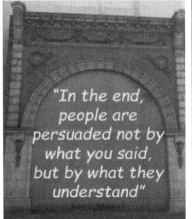

How to Win The Next USA Presidential Campaign	How Trump Won
Teddy Goff explains how audiences process and use social media	A two-part SOSTAC® Analysis of How Trump Won from Situation Analysis to Strategy, Tactics, Action and Control

prsmith.org/blog

How do customers perceive your website?
Do customers understand your web site? There are many ways to find this answer. **Usability Testing** shows how users attempt to complete specific tasks. An observer watches how easy or difficult it is to complete various tasks. See the 'Control' section which shows how this testing keeps you in control of your site – without it – your site might be out of control and damaging your brand as users become frustrated as they fail to complete their tasks.

More In-Depth approaches also measure eye-movement, heart beats and sweat to determine whether users are stimulated by various sections of a web site (see p.76). Meanwhile **Session Maps and Heat Maps** (see below) are used to try to understand how customers process information on a website.

These session maps record an individual's eye movements across a web page (erratic/random eye movement suggests confusion). The larger the circle (see below) the more time spent looking.

Session Map courtesy of www.etre.com

The results of all the individual Session Maps are then aggregated to generate a single Heat Map (see next page) with warmer colours revealing areas most looked at and 'black' indicating no one looked at this part of the page (in this case no one noticed the 'Sale' sign).

Heat Map courtesy of www.etre.com

That's probably why most organizations put their brand top left. Incidentally the eye movement used to be an 'F', starting top left, scanning across, reverting to top left and then scanning down and across (to complete the top two rows of the 'F').

Mobile Experience Heat Map courtesy of App Analytics

Lower Conversions on Mobile

Research suggests that conversion rates for visitors using mobiles is a lot lower than if they were using laptops or PCs. They're typically between one half and one third of those on desktop (Chaffey 2018). How visitors hold their phones affects how easy it is to click various parts of the screen. CTAs (Calls To Action) must be easily accessible.

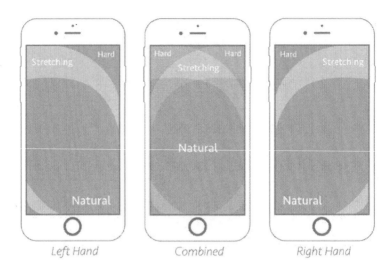

Left Hand   Combined   Right Hand

This summary suggests a 'best practice' design of screen interaction points, i.e. calls-to-action (CTAs) should focus in the natural green areas (in the centre) and avoid the red 'hard areas' (on the extreme top and bottom areas). Incidentally these red areas are where the navigation menu is often located, so alternatives to this should be provided (Chaffey 2018).

Advanced UX Research: Includes Blood Sweat & Tears
Some advanced User Experience studies analyse how visitor's actually use a particular web site and benchmark it against a number of competitive sites to identify any barriers or difficulties.

They also measure how pages, tabs, images affect the user experience. Companies like Space Between, measure more than just eye movement tracking and click behaviour analysis (using classic heat maps), they also measure **emotional arousal** (and stress) through **GSR (galvanic skin response)** since sweat glands are aroused by stimuli. They use **Facial Recognition** (including how the eyebrows move) to gauge emotional reactions and they also monitor **heart rate**.

They ask visitors to think aloud (speak about how they feel) as they complete various tasks. They also measure NPS (nett promoter score. Have a look at the UX Fashion Report by Space Between (2018) which explores a typical customer journey for the UK's largest fashion provider, ASOS and benchmark it against two competitor websites, Boohoo & Zara.

It reveals interesting insights that often get missed e.g. Boohoo allows customers to proceed to checkout from any page, without forcing them to go through the basket page first.

Or another insight revealed that visitors did not like having to open an account, instead of just purchasing as a guest. Space Between (2018)

How do some videos work better than others?
Why do some videos work better than others? Which bits of your videos arouse emotion? Live research is conducted by companies who deliver Emotional Response Video Analysis. Basically, they have recruited audiences ready and waiting to watch your videos. Their reaction (including body language/facial reaction and even pupil dilation) identifies which parts of your video arouse customers and which bits don't.

This helps video makers to cut out the bland content and release the high impact video clips which increases the likelihood of the videos being liked, discussed and shared.

How do some words work better than others?
Changing a single word on a website has resulted in a
300% increase in click through rate – Microsoft once
claimed.

There is no doubt that certain words trigger far better
reactions than others. Constant Beta testing key phrases and
data analysis helps.

Which worked best?

President Obama's Digital Director, Teddy Goff, told me
that one of these statements had a much higher impact than
the other:
- 'you should be a donor'
- 'you should donate'

Which one, do you think, worked best?
Stop and think for a moment before reading the answer.

Teddy Goff discovered that people were more likely to be
persuaded by the first statement as nouns were found to be
more powerful than verbs (Lee, 2013). Sometimes we just
don't fully know why this is, but testing and analysis will
reveal which works best. Hence the importance of
developing a constant beta culture.

Do check out how changing one button on a website
boosted revenues so much that they named it The $300
Million Button.

Test 'Fully Human' v 'Nearly Human' Bots

Japanese robotics engineer, Masahiro Mori, observed (1970s) that the more human his robots appeared, the more people reacted positively towards them. But when robots look too similar to humans (but still seen as a robot) people saw them as 'visually revolting'.

This chasm between 'fully human' and 'nearly human'. is the **'The Uncanny Valley'**. More recently audiences disliked the very realistic looking Final Fantasy movie animation (some children cried). Was this the 'Uncanny Valley'? Dreamworks Studios discovered (during test screenings) that children felt the movie's almost real animations were spooky. They changed the characters to be more cartoon-like.

Sophia, the first robot to have citizenship (Saudi Arabia) has a transparent rear head, perhaps to ensure it is seen as a robot and not a human? See Sophia on video in 'Here come the clever bots' and what she says about 'evil' prsmith.org /blog

Do customers see things differently on their mobile?

What percentage of your visitors view your site on a mobile?

Stats vary, however Statista suggest that over 50% of web traffic, worldwide, comes from mobile devices (excluding tablets) (Clement 2020). How many visitors still receive a bad user experience as their big thumbs try to click tiny tabs (designed for desktop usage primarily). They then tediously expand screens with cumbersome double fingers. This is too time consuming and too inconvenient. It's an unpleasant experience.

All the analytics packages (Google, Facebook etc.) will tell you what percentage are accessing your online platforms via which devices.

What percentage of your customers read emails on a mobile?

More than 70% of people read their email via mobile (Campaign Monitor 2019).

You need to think about the content you use. Is the content mobile-friendly? Are the Calls To Action clearly visible and easily clickable on a small screen?

Thinking only about mobile is wrong

Think more about 'mobility' as opposed to 'mobile'. Think about:

what they see on your website landing page,

or how your email looks on their small screen;

the state of mind of the user and

how their environment is different to sitting in an office. In fact, it's time to start thinking about a mobile free world very soon – a hands-free **post-mobile utopian world**.

Do customers process information differently on mobile?

The UX (User Experience) on the mobile is unique as users process information differently when they are on their mobiles because they are often multi-tasking, more likely to be interrupted and the small screen size means that reading comprehension plummets. See Appendix 4 for this excellent piece: Marketing on Mobile by Goldberg way back in 2013.

Keep looking at tech developments and just like Amazon and Uber, keep asking 'how can tech help my customers?

How Uber Reduced the Customer's Cognitive Load

Once upon a time booking a taxi meant, dialing directory enquiries, asking for a cab company, dialling them, waiting, enquiring, agreeing, waiting (in the rain), cab can't find you, eventually finds you and eventually can't find the destination, haggle about the fare. Go home. End of CX.

'A common theme in disruption is that the technology already exists, the job to be done already exists, but the two have never been put together in an affordable and accessible product.' Christensen 2016
Isn't this what Uber have done?

Let's wrap up this 'How' question with 10 Great 'How' Questions from Steve Jackson (2009) Cult of Analytics. Can you answer all of these?

10 Great 'HOW' Questions

1. What are the Top 5 most important actions (conversions) that you want a visitor to take when on your website?
2. Define 'lightly engaged' vs 'heavily engaged' (visited 10 pages and spent 240+ seconds on your site). Keep an eye on these heavily engaged visitors!

3. How many clicks/pages it takes to complete the buying process and how long this process takes in seconds. This could be one set of criteria to define your segment. For example, if it takes 5 pages and 60 seconds on average, to buy a product, you could use this as engagement criteria.
4. Which sources of traffic drives 'engaged' visitors (and which key words engage more visitors)?
5. Which source of traffic results in a sale or a contract being signed?
6. What could happen after you have sold or converted - encourage visitors to buy more or to tell a friend or....?
7. How do we get people to stay on our site longer and activate them?
8. Is key content (pages or videos) being read/watched?
9. Do these pages have higher conversion rates?
10. What helps the nurturing process?

Who What Why – Summary
Behavioural Insights are very possibly the greatest untapped marketing asset. Most marketers are not exploiting the value of behavioural insights (capturing and consolidating customer behavioural data from multiple channels in a single database).

Despite newly automated processes (marketing automation), marketers are increasingly capturing this data, but not using it to build better marketing campaigns (Forrester, 2013).

Cookies, digital body language, big data and marketing automation collect a lot of useful customer data.

It is possible that with rigorous detailed analytics, specific rules, deep understanding of customers and careful planning, a marketer can give customers much more relevant content and experiences whilst automating many marketing activities to boost results.

There's a brief explanation of How Cookies, Digital Body Language, Big Data and Marketing Automation Help You To Know Your Customer in Appendix 5.

Keep Asking Great Questions
How can data add value to the CX?
What do we have to do to deliver the best lifetime CX?

All traffic is not equal
Those visitors that stay a few seconds, or move through the steps in your shopping cart, or enter your lead generation process, are more valuable to you than visitors who see your page for a few seconds and leave.'
(Steve Jackson, Cult of Analytics).

Stop wasting time on the stuff that doesn't help you.

'Stop wasting time on the stuff that doesn't help you.' Steve Jackson

Web analytics allows you to segment or filter visitors based on certain criteria but in a different way to the way marketers segment via demographic or psychographic data.

You can set up a web analytics tool to view how visitors from a certain country, or city, act on your website as compared to everyone else and see if there are differences. You can segment (filter) by (a) Marketing campaign to see what's converting best, (b) Unpaid traffic sources (referring websites), (c) Location; device; search phrase; site behaviour (engage); converters; visitor loyalty (segment by repeat visits, recency and frequency) and more. Steve Jackson (2011)

Create a business culture that 'craves customer knowledge'. Create an A/B culture (of split testing). Create a 'constant beta' culture. Always optimizing.
Always improving by half a percent here and there can have a big impact on the bottom line.

Will you be successful?
Asking great questions is one indicator of both your organization's and your own, future success.

Think customers first
Bring an empty chair to every meeting. Amazon boss, Jeff Bezos, brings an empty chair to meetings to remind everyone of the omnipresence of the customer.

Early on Bezos brought an empty chair into meetings so lieutenants would be forced to think about the crucial participant who wasn't in the room: the customer.

Now that surrogate's role is played by specially trained employees, dubbed "Customer Experience Bar Raisers." When they frown, vice presidents tremble. Rule no. 2 of Amazon boss, Jeff Bezos's 10 Leadership Lessons (Anders, 2012).

Ask: 'Why Do You Have A Website?'
They can be expensive to create, maintain and service. They can also damage your brand if not managed carefully. The primary reason why you have a website is simply: To Help Customers.

Ok, so that's the Customer Analysis section (Who, Why and How).

It's easy now to see how **"Our competitive advantage is understanding our customer, better than our competitors"** (source unknown).

Now let's explore competitors i.e. how you go about analyzing your competitors.

1.2 Competitor Analysis

You have to know your competitors. Who are they? What are their strengths and weaknesses. How do they compete against you? How do you compete against them? Do you play to your strengths? What is your competitive advantage (from your customers' point of view).

Part of your competitor analysis explores your organization's strengths and weaknesses (compared to your competitors). The external analysis, on the other hand, includes opportunities and threats (both direct and indirect) in the external market place, such as trends and competitor strategies and tactics. You probably refer to all of this as a SWOT analysis.

So, here are some competitor questions you must answer:

- How good are your competitors' websites?
- How good are your competitor's social media platforms?
- What social content works for your competitors?
- What Facebook content works for your competitors?
- What customers say about your competitors?
- What keywords work best in your competitors' ppc ads?
- What inbound links are your competitors using?
- Do you have enough share of voice?
- How big is your competitor's marketing team and budget?
- What are people saying about your competitors?
- Who are your new content marketing competitors?
- Are competitor's embracing technology shifts (big data, MA, AI, IoT, VR & AR) better than you?

Hyper-Competition

Firstly, a warning: your business has moved into an environment packed with Hyper Competition. You have new, indirect competitors who compete with you for your customers' attention using content marketing. You are also in a borderless market with competitors from all over the world. You are also in a category-less market with competitors from other business sectors trying to acquire your customers. IoT (internet of Things) will accentuate this.

Once upon a time, supermarkets sold groceries and petrol stations sold petrol. Today supermarkets sell petrol as well as pet insurance, BBQs and clothes, while petrol stations now also sell groceries, DVDs, fresh coffee, internet connection and more.

We live in a category-less world determined by strength of brand and the ability to grow via share of wallet (selling a wider range to the same customer) rather than just share of market. Does the iWatch compete with Samsung, Swatch or Amazon? Can the big platform companies like Google, Facebook, Amazon or BAT (Baidu, Alibaba or Tencent) move into any market they choose?

Hyper-Competition In Your Pocket
Amazon and eBay mobile apps compete with all retailers. The apps invite customers, while in a competitor's retail store, to scan in a product to see how much cheaper they can get it via the app (plus they deliver it to your door). Plus, there are many other 'price comparison apps'.

So, retailers have to have even better apps (that add value rather than compete on price) to compete inside your hypercompetitive pocket. Meanwhile Amazon can target ads at customers within a radius of one mile of a competing store.

'If a retailer is not motivating people
to use its app in-store,
their customers may use a competitor's instead.'
(Gray, 2013)

Hyper-Competition Hits High Street Burger Chains

We know you are going to go to Burger King because you tweeted "going to #BurgerKing". Competitors that are monitoring and data mining real-time conversations can offer you McDonald's coupons just as you arrive at Burger King's door.

Hyper-Competition in the Watch Market
Apple sold more watches than the entire Swiss Watch Industry last year (ThisIsMney.com 2020).

Illegal Hyper-Competition

Some competition is legal and some is not so legal: <u>Premier League to Clamp Down on illegal Streams after 30,000 Sites Taken Down Last Year</u> – but it's still competition. 30,000 illegal competitors! Digital markets attract digital competition both legal and illegal. I have illegal competitors trying to market SOSTAC® templates!

Hyper-Competitive Ads

Both Facebook and LinkedIn enable competitors to target their ads by age, interests, location or company. They can even target their ads at your employees (LinkedIn), your fans (Facebook) and even your website visitors (Google and other ad networks).

Hyper-Competitive Content Wars

Customers are drowning in a rising sea of marketing content yet many marketers don't know why some content works and some fails. This creates a situation that 'leads to more content being created.' (Belicove, 2013)

Drowning in a sea of content

Every two days we create as much information as we did in the last two thousand years. Eric Schmidt, CEO Google effectively said this back in 2010 (Kirkpatrick 2010). That was ten years ago. Today, we are all drowning in a sea of content.

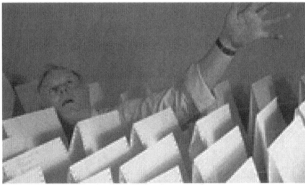

We are all drowning in a sea of content

As customers' attention spans shrink, email open rates plummet and social media engagement nosedives, the information fatigued, multi-tasked, semi-burnt out customer has limited time and desire to give their personal data to 'other' companies. So, first in wins (first to get the sign ups wins). The 'connected customer' expects the 'Internet of Everything' (everything connected) to deliver highly relevant, added value content and experiences constantly.

Competitor Web Site Traffic Analysis

You can monitor your competitor's website traffic, favorite pages, inbound links, key phrases, key phrases that work in organic search, phrases that work in online ads, and so much more. You can also find your competitors' customers and prospects attending a conference or an event (even a competitor's conference or event). You can even identify competitors' customers, e.g. if you are in the enterprise software business you can identify users of certain types of enterprise software from the enterprise software's tracking code used on their websites.

How good are your competitors' websites?

There are many competitor monitoring services such as Alexa.com which reveal information about most sites' traffic, including: bounce rate; most popular content; key phrases used; audience profile; daily pages views; daily duration; where visitors come from; inbound links. Paid subscriptions also get demographics including location, age and gender. Other services like Experian's Hitwise.com not only reveal insights into competitor's search, affiliates, display and social marketing strategies, they also:

- profile who visits your competitors' sites
- identify what is driving competitors' success
- benchmark the effectiveness of your existing customer acquisition strategies
- measure your website's performance against your competitors.

SimilarWeb allows you to compare website traffic stats, what your competitors are doing right and wrong, how to use this information to your advantage. The free version gives you all of the information below:

- Number of visitors (weekly in last 6 months)
- Duration (average)
- Page Views
- Bounce Rate
- Traffic Channel Sources include: direct, referrals (incl. breakdown) sites, search (incl. breakdown), social (incl. breakdown), mail and display
- Audience Geography, which geographic sources they come from
- Audience Interests: what other topics (incl. a topic word cloud), categories and websites these visitors also visited
- Website Ranking (global, within a country and by category)
- Keywords used to find the site (organic search and paid search)
- Similar Sites

The pro version includes: most popular pages, date range options, more details and more licensed seats (more of your team can use it).

In addition, you can commission the advanced research mentioned on p.76, ie a tailored report analysing the CX (UX) on your own site compared to your competitors' sites.

> **'Find new customers by profiling who visits competitive sites.'** Steve Jackson, Cult of Analytics (2011)

How good are your competitors' social media?
A social media audit identifies which platforms your competitors are using, how frequently, what kind of content, how many followers and engagement level.

What   content works for your competitors?
Research agencies can benchmark audience size, engagement, content that's popular and a lot more. SimilarWeb.com, SEMRush.com and others can benchmark your business against your competitors.

What are people saying about your competitors?
Social listening tools let you hear what is being said about your brand and your competitors' brands and staff, as well as who is saying it. Social listening tools (many of which are free) allow you to drill down and engage in these conversations.

This process of listening really helps you to develop your content strategy because you can listen to real needs being discussed and also what works for your competitors may well work for you also.

Many **social listening tools** are discussed on my blog post, 'Social Listening Skills Part 1' which includes everything from free Google Alerts to other tools that monitor mentions (on the major social media platforms), to full blown sentiment analysis that collects all mentions of a brand and calculates a single score reflecting the positive or negative mood or sentiment.

Welcome to the world of Infonomics

Information has evolved from being a business by product to a business performance fuel, and now to an accepted form of legal tender. Organizations that cultivate, manage and are prepared to leverage this new-age currency, increasingly have an array of revenue streams and commercial options available to them. 'Welcome to the world of infonomics.' (Laney, 2014)

What keywords work best in your competitors' ads?
Eliminate bad keywords that waste your money. SpyFu finds your competitors' most successful ad copy which saves you spending time testing. It also helps you to 'weed out money-wasting keywords with negative match suggestions'. This also reveals your competitors' keyword strategies including every keyword they've bought on Adwords, every organic rank, and every ad variation in the last 6 years. Watch this 8 minute video 'Build Winning PPC Ad Copy Part 2, Spyfu Ad History' on YouTube.

What inbound links are your competitors using?
To see your competitors' inbound links, go to: Moz Open Site Explorer   www.opensiteexplorer.org and insert their name or their brand.

Remember competition is only one click away.

Do you have enough share of voice (SOV)?
SOV can mean different things e.g. SOV PPC Ads, SOV PR/editorial, SOV SEO. PPC people see SOV as a share of

the total amount of impressions available to buy on a search or display platform whereas PR people see SOV as brand mentions out of all brand mentions in that sector. 'Mentions, segmented by vertical (social, news, blogs, etc.) often filtered by sophisticated Boolean queries that associate brand terms with keywords' (Weintraub, 2013). SOV SEO calculates how much traffic a brand can get for a particular key phrase as a percentage of all traffic generated for that same phrase. See 'Control' section for more on SOV.

How big is your competitor's marketing team and budget (and how good are they)?
A more manual approach involves a LinkedIn search on your competitor's name and any job titles that contain 'marketing', digital marketing' or 'communications'. The search produces an immediate list giving an initial indication of the size of the marketing department. Many researchers temporarily change their privacy restrictions to make their searches anonymous.

Many other companies only keep a small marketing team while subcontracting the marketing to external agencies.

Amazon v Sears (going out of business?)

Sears was the largest retailer in the USA but over 10 years Sears lost 96% market value ($28b to $1b) while Amazon gained nearly 2000% ($18b to £355b).

Sears 'has not made the shift to digital' (Business Insider report). Bond traders are betting sears will go out of business in two years (Bukhari 2017).

Excellent digital competitors think differently e.g. Amazon ask: 'How can we use technology to help the customer? How can we make it easier?' E.g. where and when do you most need to re-order washing-up liquid?

Answer: When you squeeze the bottle and realise it's almost empty!

Enter the 'Dash Button' – a small device that fits onto walls, cupboards etc. Set it up with your mobile and then just push it when you need to
renew a particular product. Amazon then despatch it.

Although the dash button was withdrawn last year (Fox Rubin 2019), it was arguably the original IoT Smart device designed to help customers save time. Part of Amazon's relentless quest to help customers via technology wherever possible.

Although Amazon's 'Dash' button has been discontinued (Fox Rubin 2019), it is perhaps one of the original IoT smart home devices that helped customers save time.

Your Competitive Advantage

Knowing your own strengths and weaknesses is obviously important. So why do your customers buy from you rather than your competitor?

Defining your competitive advantage (in the eyes of your customers) summarizes almost everything we've covered up to now.

So why do your customers buy from you (instead of your competitors and vice versa)?

Is there a specific, distinctive, reason?
Is it because you are:

- Technically Better
- Different product functions
- Looks Pleasing
- Tastier

- More Reliable
- Built To Last Longer
- More Easily Serviced
- Better Service Support
- More Flexible
- Faster Delivery
- More Mobile
- Readily Available
- Better Priced
- Better Brand
- Other Reason?

or

- You respond faster
- You respond to discussions online
- You have a presence online (all main channels)
- You have a lot of added value online
- Or maybe you just happened to be in the right place at the right time?
- Or perhaps there is an emotional reason?

---

6 Crunch Competitive Questions

What is the best benefit of our product from customers' view?

How is our product/service completely unique?

Why would a customer buy from us and not competition?

When will the customer be better off buying from someone else?

List attributes and categorize as appealing to logic or emotion of customer. How hard is it to understand the attribute?

(Steve Jackson, 2009)

Competitive Advantage 'The 3 Circle Model' by Urbany and Davis (2007)

Now here's the very simple, yet enlightening, Urbany and Davis 3 circle model. This is the most intriguing insight I have come across in the last 20 years.

Consider the 3 core concepts of Company, Customers and Competition.

This is the Customer Circle (on the next page). It represents the value sought by the customer – the requirements and benefits that they seek. These requirements and benefits may include deeper values.

The value sought
by the customer –
the requirements
& benefits
that they seek.

Customer Circle

Essentially the Customer Circle represents what the customer wants or what value the customer is seeking.

The second circle is your Company Circle. It represents the value customers perceive, or think, you offer to them.

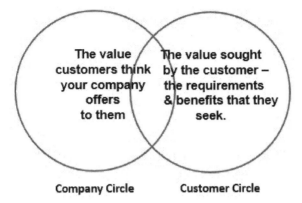

Company Circle   Customer Circle

Area 1 (on the next page), the overlapping area in the middle, is Positive Value. This is the value you are perceived to deliver to satisfy customer needs.

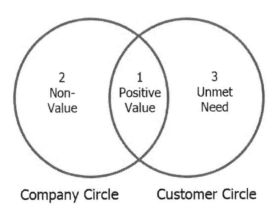

Company Circle   Customer Circle

Area 2 is 'Non-Value', which Urbany and Davis describe as 'the product or service you produce that the customer either doesn't care about, or perhaps, doesn't know about.'

Area 3 is called 'Unmet Need'. Urbany and Davis describe this as customer needs that are not satisfied by your products and services and hence they offer a possible future growth opportunity.

The third circle (on the next page) is called the Competitor Circle. This is the final piece of the jigsaw. It soon opens up a whole new way of thinking......

The competitor circle represents what value does the customer perceive in your competitor's offering.

You can see it's a Venn diagram (next page).

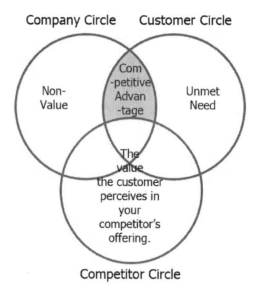

The overlapping shaded area at the top is 'the pure definition of competitive advantage'. As Urbany and Davis say, this is the value that you create that matters to customers, but, that is different to competition. This is why people choose us.'

Do you know why customers choose you? Do the reasons change over time?

So the next big question for you is **'What's your competitive advantage?'**

This excellent question forces you to begin the process of defining your distinctive competitive advantage. If you ask six different members of your team, you might get six different answers.

You can share Professor Joe Urbany's approach to Competitive Strategy and watch the 3 min video on prsmith.org/blog (Select: 'Beware: Customers See Your Competitive Advantage Differently'

They never saw it coming

They never saw it coming. Hidden competitors lurk. Spirit level manufacturers never imagined that they might one day compete with phones or free spirit level apps.

Now this category-less, indirect, competitor is eating into their business. So relentless improvement is required as new (direct and indirect competitors) continually emerge.

See how wonderfully disruptive 'digital sizzle' can be in the Objectives section.

1.3 Partners/CoMarketers and Intermediaries

Your Situation Analysis should also include an analysis of your partners to see which works best whether they are intermediaries (e.g. retailers) or other strategic alliances (marketing marriages) giving you new routes to market. Some organisations consider strategic partners as long term strategic decisions (see 'Strategy' section). Others see partners as more tactical elements of 'Place' (or distribution), while others consider partners to be the 8th P when talking about the marketing mix.

Partners/CoMarketers require resources e.g. clear communications to manage, measure and nurture partner relationships, hence some organizations recognize this and have partner managers and partnership directors managing many different types of partners:

- Intermediaries – such as price comparison sites or aggregators
- Affiliates – your network of sites that promote your product (or that link to your website)
- Influencers – your network of bloggers, journos, tweeters
- Marketing Marriages/Strategic Alliances – whose brands add value to each other's customers and target audiences overlap – sharing databases or campaign costs.
- Link partners – partners who help to boost your SEO
- Syndication partners – partners who will share content online
- Advertising partners – whose sites share ad space in the long-term

- Is it worth maintaining all of these partners? Or should you reallocate your resources? Your Partnership Analysis will tell you.

Copetitors

Today, it is not uncommon for some of your partners (or even customers) to compete with you on some of their portfolio of products/services. We call these 'copetitors'. Perhaps some of your competitors may partner with you on some of your other products/services?

So your partnership analysis should identify what works and what doesn't, or at least what is restricting success, so that it can be fixed.

1.4 Competencies Analysis

Your Performance or Results Analysis will already indicate some of your strengths and weaknesses. However, it's good to know these before you start spending your budget and the results start coming in.

Here's a nice quick Digital Marketing Capability Analysis which you can take any time you are ready to face the reality of where you are, or your organization is, in terms of digital competencies.

It explores your Digital Marketing Competencies in 7 aspects using a score from 1-5 (5 being 'Optimized').

1. Your Strategic approach
2. Evaluation and performance improvement process
3. Management buy-in to investment in digital marketing
4. Resourcing and structure for digital including integration
5. Data and infrastructure or platforms
6. Integrated customer communications across Paid-Owned-Earned media
7. Integrated customer experiences across desktop and mobile devices

Ask yourself 'are these strengths or weaknesses?'.
Knowing your strengths and weaknesses is essential in business.
Now consider Smart Insights' Digital Marketing Capability Analysis. It helps you to know where your organization is in terms of digital transformation steps or stages.

Stage 1
'Initial' (with no strategy, no KPIs etc.)

Stage 2
'Managed' (with prioritized activities and some KPIs etc.)

Stage 3
'Defined' (with clearly defined vision & strategy, Quality bases KPIs, partial integration of data and systems etc.)

Stage 4
'Quantified' (KPIs with weighted attribution, integrated systems etc.)

Stage 5
'Optimized' (Lifetime Value KPIs, integral part of strategy etc.).

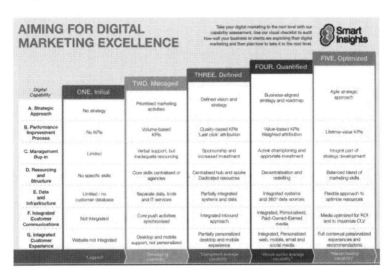

Apologies for the very small print. It is too small to read. You will find this 'Digital Marketing Capability Analysis' in the bibliography also under Smart Insights. There is also a table on the next page with more legible text.

Obviously an 'Optimized' organization has a competitive advantage over an organization that is only at the 'Initial' stage of its digital marketing maturity.

Digital Transformation requires many skills (as well as the technology). On the next page we show the 5 steps to becoming fully digitally transformed.

NB This matrix was adopted from the original Carnegie Mellon Capability Maturity model for systems (CMMI) to become the Capability Maturity Model Integration (adapted by Dave Chaffey of Smart Insights).

Stage → Criteria ↓	1. Initial (Directionless)	2. Managed	3. Defined (Structured Testing)	4. Quantified (Customer- centric)	5. Optimised
A. Strategic Approach	No Strategy	Prioritised Marketing Activities	Defined Vision & Strategy	Whole Business- aligned	Agile Strategic Approach
B. Performance Improvement Process	No KPIs	Volume Based KPIs	Quality Based KPIs +Last Click Attribution AB tests + CTAs	Value Based KPIs +Weighted Attribution Multivariate Testing	Lifetime Value KPIs
C. Management By-In	Limited	Verbal Support but inadequate Resourcing	Sponsorship & Increased Investment	Active Championing & Full Investment	Integral Part of Strategy Development
D. Resourcing & Structure	No specific skills	Core Skills Centralised or agencies	Centralised Hub + Dedicated Resources	Decentralising & Reskilling	Balanced Blend of Marketing Skills
E. Data & Infrastructure	Limited/No Customer Database	Separate Data, Tools & IT Services	Partially Integrated Systems & Data Mktg Automation Remarketing	Integrated Systems & 360 Data Sources Social CRM	Flexible Approach To Optimise Resources 360 customer view
F. Integrated Customer Comms	Not Integrated	Core Push Activities Synchronised	Integrated Inbound Approach	Integrated, Personalised, Paid Owned Earned	Constant Optimisation to Help Customers & Max CLV & ROI
G. Integrated Customer Experience	Web Site Not Integrated	Desktop & Mobile Support Not Personalised	Partially Personalised Experience 90 day planning programme of testing	Integrated Personalised, web, email Social Ads +Realtime social media & Shared CX	Full Contextual Personalised Experiences & Recommendatio ns

The Capability Maturity Model Integration for planning your Digital Transformation (adapted by Dave Chaffey)

The strategic choice which then emerges is whether to build a newly structured marketing department or employ external agencies. The Strategy section will mention this again and you can ALSO see a newly structured marketing department in the 'Action' section.

1.5 Performance/Results Analysis

The results of all your efforts are summarized by the Key Performance Indicators (KPIs).

They never lie.

Never look at numbers in isolation (particularly when looking at results). We need to see them in the context of previous periods (to see if there is a trend) and also we need to see them compared to competition to see how we have performed comparatively.

For example, £10m sales is great news if we only made £5m last year. But if we made £20m last year then it's terrible news. But what if the market had shrunk from £100m to £20m? Our market share would have increased from 10% (£10m/£100m) to 25% (£5/£20m).

The next strategic question is do we want to stay in a market this size? We'll look at strategy later. Meanwhile here's a selection of typical KPIs which can be used to analyze performance.

Objectives

KPI	Results Previous Period	Objective Current Period	Results Current Period filled in later (in the Control section)
ROI (Return On Investment)			
Sales - units - value			
Market Share - units - value			
Market Leader Number (in top 5)			
Awareness Level (offline survey)			
Preference Level (offline survey)			
NPS Score (Net Promoter Score)			
Sentiment Score (incl. competitor comparison)			

Website/Blog
  Unique Visitors
  Average Duration
  Subscribers to Newsletter
  Leads generated			

Objectives (contd.)

KPI	Results Previous Period	Objective Current Period	Results Current Period filled in later
Cost Per Visitor (website)			
Cost Per Like (Facebook)			
Cost Per Lead			
Cost Per Customer Acquisition			
Cost Per Customer Retention			
Database Size			
Prospects/Leads			
Customers			
Advocates			
Influencers			

Specific Website KPIs

KPI	Results Previous Period	Objective Current Period	Results Current Period
Site Visits			
Unique Visitors			
Bounce Rate			
Duration			

Website KPIs contd.	Results Previous Period	Objective Current Period	Results Current Period
Page Views passive engagement			
Most Popular Page(s)/downloads			
Engagement - Downloads			
Engagement - Likes/Favorites			
Engagement - Comments			
Engagement - Shares			
Engagement - Registrations/			
Churn Rate			
Conversions Leads & Sales			
Sales (all sales)			
Task Completion			
SCAR (Shopping Cart Abandonment Rate)			
Satisfaction Score			
NPS Score			
Sentiment Score			
Share of Voice			
Social Media Platforms			
Followers/Likes – engagement etc.			

There are many different approaches, to KPI desktops, layouts…

The next approach turns the pyramid upside down and into the sales funnel, starting with number of visitors, % engagement and sales.

The basic sales funnel

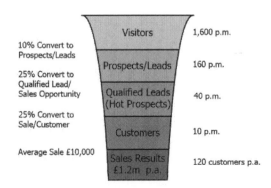

An organization's performance can also be summarized by its Sales Funnel

You will see how the sales funnel and all of the KPIs can be used to set crystal clear objectives, in chapter 2, Objectives.

Beware Of Bad Stats:
Correlation Is Not Causation

'Have you ever noticed how we only win the World Cup under a Labour government?' British Prime Minister Harold Wilson, once said with tongue in cheek.

Or 37% of people who have a coffee mug with their company logo on it have been promoted within the last 6 months, compared to 8% of those people who did not have a coffee mug with their company logo on it. Yes, it's OK to count these things, but I doubt that there's any statistical significance or association between owning a mug with a logo and getting promoted. Correlation is not causation.

1.6 Market Trends – opportunities and threats

In the Customer Analysis section I mentioned some trends in the way customers digest information – shorter attention spans, more visual, multi-tasking, mobile etc.
In addition, every market has its own specific trends that affect the market.

The PEST factors (political, economic, social and technological) or PESTED (add environment and demographics), need to be monitored to identify trends that can affect your business either as an opportunity or a threat.

1.6.1 Politics

BREXIT & TRUMP
The political shift of Britain and Northern Ireland leaving the EU will have a significant effect on any business trading in this area. . Similarly, trade-wars triggered by new Donald Trump policies will affect any businesses marketing within these regions.

GDPR
The General Data Privacy Regulations are already having a major impact on all organisations in Europe and any organisations doing business with European customers.

Global increase in cyber attacks

World's largest hack in 2013, reported by Yahoo! in 2016

See prsmith.org/blog for GDPR Impact

Some markets need more regulation than others such as alcohol, tobacco, medication. Without regulations, some markets could damage customer safety and health.

Do some markets need more regulation than others?

1.6.2 Economics

Politics and economics are interwoven. Obviously al organisations have to respond and plan according to economic cycles whether it is, for example, a peak pushing prices up or a trough pushing prices down.

Interestingly, the front page of the Economist, recently announced that 'The World's most valuable resource is no longer oil, but data.' Data has become the lifeblood of any business. We cannot survive without it. Data (or lack of) can destroy a business. How long could you continue without access to your data? Data can create competitive advantage.

Industrial giants such as GE and Siemens now promote themselves as data firms.

Economist.com

Data has value
Companies will be, in the future, partly valued by the scale and quality of their data as well as their ability to mine it.

You don't own your own daughter's data
The father of the 14 year old Molly Russell who tragically died recently, bravely requested his daughter's data so that they can see what she was looking at just before she died to stop this content ever being used again. Instagram (owned by facebook) own that data – not the parents. See the brave

plea on BBC TV by the father for access to his daughter's data and further updates
(Hurynag 2020)

Customer data is everywhere

And we leave it everywhere. We leave digital trails when we browse, click, scan or fill in a form. This data can be cross referenced with social media platforms to gather extra data. Additional third party databases can be used to layer on more information. Search, social, and analytics can be combined with some clever APIs (Application Programming Interfaces) which help software components to interact with each other.

Big Data is everywhere

Big Data refers to relatively large amounts of structured and unstructured data that require machine-based systems and technologies in order to be fully analyzed. 'The much-hyped term has inspired a slew of definitions, many of which involve the concepts of massive volume, velocity and variety of information. In other words, what turns data into.' (Kaye 2013).

Big Data is everywhere
Here are 10 Useful Ways Big Data Is Used – That You Probably Didn't Know – from Lady Gaga To Premature Babies See prsmith.org/blog

---

Data storage costs keep falling

As the cost of data storage comes tumbling down and data integration/analysis tools get cleverer, potentially large volumes of useful customer data is emerging almost everywhere.

1.6.3 Social

Us humans have shorter attention spans, less time, become information fatigued and also, visually driven, with perhaps social media paranoia as 1 in 4 suffer from mental health issues in the UK. We seem to need to be connected 24/7 to brands, people, experiences and some of us even sleep with our phones! This wonderful satirical piece below actually reveals a lot about us, and, in particular, the new generations coming through.

Miracle Teenager Survives On His Own For Almost 6 Hours With No Wi-Fi

IN what has been hailed as 'a miracle', one Waterford teenager has reportedly survived in his home with no connection to the internet for almost 6 whole hours.

WATERFORDWHISPERSNEWS.COM

WaterfordWhispersNews.com

Alongside the customers' growing need for connectivity, we find other trends, some more surprising than others:

- Customer Service Is Falling
- Customer Trust is Falling

- Customer Rage Is Rising
- Customer Attention Spans Are Shrinking
- Customer Have Less Time
- Customer Patience Is Falling
- Customer Feedback Is Falling

Customer Service is Falling

75% of customers believe it takes too long to reach a live agent while more than 66% end up hanging up in frustration. 67% of customers hung up the phone out of frustration they could not talk to a real person. Lobo 2017 Do you think these figures have improved since then?

Customer Trust Is Falling

Two-thirds of the 28 countries surveyed in the Edelman Trust Barometer has revealed that the general population did not trust the four institutions to "do what is right". This means 'people's trust has declined' Harrington (2017). Pew Research (Gramlich 2019) shows further decline of trust in Young Americans.

Customer Rage Is Rising

Consumers and advertisers are at war.

Consumers surrender their personal information which is then 'collected and sold back to advertisers for a "capitalist micro-assault [that] is, from all directions at all waking moments ... getting much more intense, focused, targeted, unyielding and galactically more boring", Doug Coupland's apocalyptic words (2015).

Customer Attention, Patience & Time Is Falling

With Attention spans shrinking (from 42 to 4 seconds) in roughly 50 years and people having so much more 'to do' via their mobile apps (& other activities), it may follow that people's patience is shrinking.

Customer Feedback Is Falling
Less trust in government, brands and professions, and survey fatigue. A typical Pew Research telephone survey customer response rate fell from 36% to just 9% over approximately 10 years to 2016. The possible causes for the general decline in feedback response rates includes: 'less trust in government, brands and professions, and survey fatigue.'
Bolling & Smith 2017

How to get more feedback
The organizations where we see quality feedback still being received are the ones that act on that feedback. Some of the best organizations go even further. They get back to those who gave the feedback and tell them that the problem has been fixed. That's the type of feedback loop we require. McGovern 2017

Does Convenience Beat Trust and Privacy?
Us, time-poor people, say we value our privacy (data), yet time-saving convenience seems to be more important. Here's Gerry McGovern (2019): 'Adweek reported on a survey which asked U.S. adults how they would trust 100 of the biggest brands with their personal data in exchange for "more relevant offers, goods and services". **Facebook ranked last.** A 2018 Honest Data poll found that **U.S. citizens think Facebook is worse for society than McDonalds or Walmart**. The only company ranked worse than Facebook was Marlboro. A 2018 CB Insights survey asked **which company will have a net negative for society 10 years from now?** "The answer was pretty overwhelmingly **Facebook.**" 'Any yet ... And yet ... **Facebook revenue rose** to $16.9 billion in the last three months of 2018, up 30%. **Monthly active users rose** to

2.32 billion, up 9%. Consequently, Facebook's **share price soared** more than 13%' (McGovern 2019). Is time a more valuable currency than privacy? Are we so time-poor that we just don't pay attention to our data use or abuse?

1.6.4 Technology

The **IoT** (Internet of Things), **AI** (Artificial Intelligence including bots), **Big Data**, **Marketing Automation**, **VR & AR** (Virtual Reality) & (Augmented Reality) are 5 big digital developments or trends to watch.

After the fixed internet of the 1990s, came the mobile internet of the 2000s connecting 2-6 billion. Then came the IoT connecting 28 billion things from smartphones, to watches, glasses, cars, clothes, your home, and your business. Jankowski (2014) suggests that 'Product sectors is where the Internet of Things Really Matters'. IoT connects chips, sensors, software, networks and data to products like your golf clubs; fridges, houses and offices.

IoT Adds Value
You can now attach, tiny chips connected via WiFi to databases and big data to products and services to deliver added value experiences to customers (such as a golf club with sensors/video & chips, connected via wifi to your phone or screen at home where you can see an analysis of your swing alongside your actual swing on screen).

We can attach rich layers of data, information, advice, tips, visuals, virtual experiences, added value to anything. This is the IoT. Tomorrow's smart products can add so much value, they can even   create new services by helping customers in new and previously, unimagined ways. IoT will shift many products into a new categories as smart products deliver additional benefits, way beyond the original products.

Smart Handbags

Real-time digital interactions with smart products means brands can get to know consumers better, amplifying and responding to their emotions. Net result consumers feel more connected to the brand and feel a greater affinity

'Customers scan the bag's unique code, with their smartphone. Based on real time, contextual data and unique product identity, the customers start getting a personalised 'surprise and delight' relationship with the brand. Everthng (2017),

---

IoT Reduces costs
e.g. Predictive Maintenance - Caterpillar maintenance analytics using machine learning   as the value of measuring and recording as much as possible becomes clear. relationships about relationships about relationships."
Fleet of 8 ships Data collected from ship-board sensors identify the correlation between the amount of money spent on cleaning, and performance improvement – saves \$3.2m pa across 8 ships.

Two Big Inevitable IoT Questions

IoT smart products will transcend traditional products across traditional product categories, boundaries and borders until we face these two big questions:

What business am I in?
What is my competitive advantage?
Forming alliances with strategic IoT partners makes sense (see strategy section).

SECURITY WARNING!

Beware – the weakest link in any integrated systems, allows hackers into your system (currently, 70% of office printers are vulnerable).

AI & Super AI

The 21st century will achieve 20,000 times the progress of the 20th century. The highly rated, American Futurist, **Ray Kurzweil** suggests that the progress of the entire 20th century would have been achieved in only 20 years at the rate of advancement in the year 2000 - in other words, by 2000, the rate of progress was 5 times faster than the average rate of progress during the 20th century.

Kurzweil believes that another 20th century's worth of progress happened between 2000 and 2014 &
that another 20th century's worth of progress will happen by 2021, in only 7 years.

A couple decades later, he believes a 20th century's worth of progress will happen multiple times in the same year, and even later, in less than one month. This is the **Law of Accelerating Returns.** Kurzweil believes that the 21st century will achieve 20,000 times the progress of the 20th century! So embrace technology developments.

So, we'll see all sorts of AI developments – the most immediate might be better chatbots! Better bots simply help customers, in a conversational way, to find answers more quickly and therefore boost conversions. They help customers to 'get the job done'.

With 2.5 billion customers using instant messaging [IM] (Economist 2016) on facebook, Whatsapp and China's WeChat (et al) an opportunity opens. Within a couple of years IM will reach about half of humanity i.e. 3.6 billion, (The Economist 2016). Today, chatbots using direct messaging are being integrated into social media channels and customer service channels.

Social Chat App + Bot = Business!

WeChat offers a prime example of how 'the place to be selling is on Facebook or Whatsapp rather than simply on web pages'). Taking the example of a restaurant, a user can read the menu, order and pay through the app. Indeed, it has been so successful that 40% of mobile transactions in China are through WeChat. (Lobo 2017).

WARNING!
Not all chatbots are equal – some hinder & some help

Some chatbots will damage your business with 70% of customer questions not being answered (The Register 2017).

However, 'good chatbots' are painstakingly built using decision trees to cover all options and Natural Language Processing (NLP) to identify the customer's real intent behind the questions, followed by rigorous testing and modifications.

AI and bots, in particular, require patience and, if building your own AI, expertise (and lots of people to set it all up).

Moving from chatbots to 'real' robots, we now see Pizza Hut Japan with robot waiters serving happy customers and also Hilton McLean Concierge bot helping customers by answering their questions. Bots will appear in all shapes and sizes.

Helpful bots will appear in all shapes and sizes.

Image by <u>Enrique Meseguer</u> from <u>Pixabay</u>

Cloud Wars

The marketing cloud is the marketing nirvana – a place, or a hub, where marketers automate and integrate all customer data, automatically analyze it then continuously and automatically serve highly relevant engaging content across multi- channels at just the right time on the right platform to the right customer.

Fast moving marketers will use the marketing cloud (multichannel marketing automation, content management tools, social media tools and analytics platforms – more later) to create a wall around their customers, which competitors will consequently find difficult to break down (particularly because of customers' changing behaviours). This is now a race towards an automated integrated digital marketing hub.

So change appears to be accelerating – whether new regulations & laws (political); or fundamental economic cycles (economics) that grow or shrink your market; shrinking attention spans (social changes); or quantum data manipulation developments (technology), the PEST factors need constant monitoring.

WARNING!

Your Animal life is Over.
Your Machine Life Has Begun.
(O'Connell 2017)

This is a powerful article from the Guardian newspaper that might make you think differently about both technology and philosophy.

The 4ᵗʰ Industrial Revolution

This is a new beginning. I know we have said this before. The Internet came along in the 1990s and we said this changes everything. It did. Then social media came along in the 'noughties' (2000s) and Newsweek announced that 'Social Media is the biggest change since the industrial revolution' (2005). And now we have even bigger changes coming via AI (Artificial Intelligence), Machine Learning, Automation and a proliferation of technology developments, economic (power) shifts, new social structures and effectively, this is it.

We are seeing the start of the 4ᵗʰ industrial revolution. With it come some wonderful opportunities and some dangerous risks.

There Has Never Been a Time of Greater Promise or Potential Peril

"The changes are so profound that, from the perspective of human history, **there has never been a time of greater promise or potential peril**. My concern, however, is that decision-makers are too often caught in traditional, linear (and non-disruptive) thinking or too absorbed by immediate concerns to **think strategically about the forces of disruption and innovation shaping our future**."

Professor Klaus Schwab, founder and executive chairman of the World Economic Forum (2018)
Schwab, K. (2018) The Fourth Industrial

Revolution, World Economic Forum

A Good or Bad Revolution?

The 4th revolution can do good or bad for both economies and societies. It could share education in new ways, reduce illness and starvation and improve the quality of life across the world. In fact, it might even alert us before national disasters occur and 'potentially also undo some of the damage wrought by previous industrial revolutions.' (Marr 2018)

On the other hand, it could further polarise the rich and the poor as low skills get low pay and high skills get much higher pay. Whilst AI creates competitive advantage between businesses, the bigger ones invest more heavily in AI to get bigger whilst wiping out, or buying, up the smaller businesses.

Marr continues: 'Some jobs will become **obsolete**. Additionally, the changes might develop so **swiftly**, that even those who are ahead of the curve in terms of their knowledge and preparation, might not be able to keep up with the ripple effects of the changes..... world governments need to plan carefully and regulate the emerging new AI capabilities to ensure our security. (Marr 2018)

Companies must invest in data tech to survive

Regardless of positive or negative 4th industrial revolution scenarios, to survive, organisations, must invest in:

[ ] Technical infrastructure and data analyzing capabilities
[ ] Staff with new data skills, that embrace new tech and are marketing orientated

[ ] Leaders capable of harnessing these dramatic business trends

Organisations that are not smart, connected organizations will soon fall behind a new wave of competition, known as Hyper-Competition, which is one of the three unstoppable business trends. Read on.

When Electricity Was Invented

Many Architects Asked The Wrong Question

Way back when electricity was invented, when some architects heard about this new invention, they thought: 'How do I add an electrical system into the buildings I'm designing? Other architects thought: 'How does electricity change the nature of the buildings I'm designing?'

The second type of architect invented the skyscraper. Before electricity, the height of buildings was limited because you couldn't efficiently move masses of people up and down countless flights of stairs. The electric lift solved that problem and opened up a whole new way to design buildings.

Companies such as Google, Amazon, Uber, and Netflix, who are thriving in this digital age, are not thriving because they are digital. They are thriving because they have adapted new models of organization that opened up as a result of digital.

McGovern 2016

Summary: Situation Analysis

So, once you thoroughly know your situation:

- Customers (who, why and how)
- Competitors (direct and indirect)
- Competencies (strengths and weaknesses)
- Market trends (opportunities and threats)
- Performance/Results (what worked and what didn't work)

You will then see what your Distinctive Competitive Advantage (DCA) is. You can then decide if this fits with what customers want now and in the future (by reading the market trends).

You can make strategic choices about whether to nurture your current DCA or develop another DCA later in the Strategy section.

Meanwhile, you must create a culture of 'customer obsession'.

You and your team must master these three big questions 'Who, Why and How'.

Listen to your customers online (as well as offline).

Get the technical infrastructure to support dynamic, cross-channel conversations with customers and the subsequent analytics to help you to find more of the same type of customers (once you know who you are after) and to help you to make better informed decisions (see Tactics section).

Finally, remember Sun Tzu's words at the start of this section:

> Those who triumph,
> Compute at their headquarters
> a great number of factors
> prior to a challenge.
>
> Those who are defeated,
> compute at their headquarters
> a small number of factors
> prior to a challenge.
>
> Much computation brings triumph.
> Little computation brings defeat.
> How much more so with no computation at all.
>
> By observing only this,
> I can see triumph or defeat.
>
> Sun Tzu

With your Situation Analysis completed you know where you really are in the marketplace. Now let's clarify where you want to go – with some realistic objectives.

Chapter 2 Objectives

Although some argue that the most important goals or objectives are simply to increase:

- Revenue
- Margin
- Customer Satisfaction
- Brand Value (controlling the brand promise increases the brand value)

I take a slightly different view and start with the ultimate objectives which are the Mission and Vision statements, followed by the typical KPIs which include the above in more detail.

2.1 Mission

This is your raison d'être (the reason your organization exists). This must include how you make the world a better place – how you ultimately help customers and stakeholders. It should also demonstrate some CSR (Corporate Social Responsibility) while giving strategic direction for the organization. Google's mission statement: 'to organize the world's information and make it universally accessible and useful' makes a lot of sense. Mission overlaps with 'a sense of purpose (see 2.6).

2.2 Vision

A vision statement is more organization orientated (as opposed to a mission statement which is more market orientated or customer/community orientated). A vision states where the organization sees itself in 3, 5 or 10 years' time. Imagine writing a headline in the New York Times or the FT for your business: 'XYZ is the number one company in the world (or Asia, China or Beijing, etc.). So the vision sets major goals for how successful your organization will be in the future. This includes size of turnover, size of organization, size of market share, local, national or global, position in the market place (number 1, 2 or 3).

After this comes the typical KPIs. Here is the KPI Pyramid (adopted from Joe Pulizzi, 2013).

A Man On The Moon

When John F. Kennedy visited NASA he met a janitor and asked him what he did. The janitor said "I'm helping to put a man on the moon". A strong mission delivers a greater shared sense of purpose for all staff.

2.3 KPIs

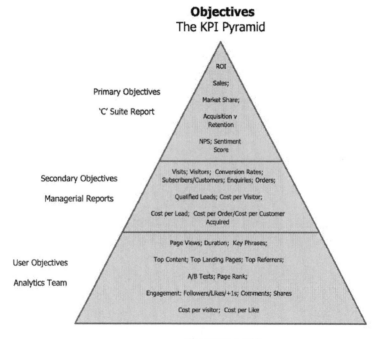

The KPI Pyramid

Key Performance Indicators can be broken down in more detail right down to revenue contribution per channel (or tool), Cost per visit/enquiry/lead/like and sale broken down by channel. Note: awareness levels, preference levels and market position are often measured via offline surveys.

You can also turn the KPI Pyramid upside down (and select fewer KPI criteria) to get the sales funnel approach to objectives. The next approach turns the pyramid upside down and into the 'sales funnel', starting with number of visitors, % engagement and eventually sales objectives.

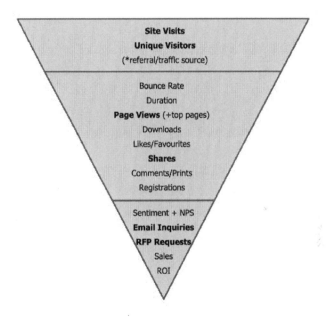

The Objectives Pyramid turned upside down
becomes a Sales Funnel

Certain click behaviour indicates whether a visitor is a prospect. It could be determined by the amount of time ('duration') they spent on specific product pages and perhaps whether they checked the price pages. A prospect can be categorized as a qualified lead if, say, they came back a second time plus watched the product demonstration video plus read some customer reviews and checked the pricing page again. So goals or objectives can be set for number of visitors, leads, qualified leads, customers and total sales revenue by using the classic sales funnel approach.

The Sales Funnel

The Sales Funnel can also be used to set objectives

If you know your conversion rates, it is easy to set objectives in terms of the number of visitors you need to generate a specific number of customers. If, for example, the sales objective is £1.2m (and the average sale is £10,000), then the organization needs 1,600 visitors each month with 10% of these becoming prospects (160 pcm). If 25% of these prospects become qualified leads (i.e. 40 qualified leads per month p.m.). If a further 25% of these qualified leads, on average, convert to becoming customers, they will get 10 new customers pcm which is 120 new customers p.a.

KPIs

You can, and should, go much deeper with your objectives. By having detailed objectives for many different KPIs (Key Performance Indicators), you have more control over your organization's performance. Here are some KPIs again.

Here is a summary list of popular KPI Objectives used online.

KPIs Objectives (some typical KPIs used online)

KPI	Q1	Q2	Q3	Q4	Tot.
Site Visits					
Unique Visitors					
Bounce Rate					
Duration					
Page Views passive engagement					
Most Popular Page/s					
Most popular downloads					
Engagement - Downloads					
Engagement - Likes/Favorites					
Engagement - Comments					
Engagement - Shares					
Engagement -					

Registrations/Newsletter					
Churn Rate (% of followers you lose)					
Conversions Leads & Sales					
Sales (all sales)					
Market Share					
ROI					
Task Completion					
Satisfaction Score					
NPS Score					
Sentiment Score					
Share of Voice					

Social Media Platforms – repeat for each one				
Followers/Like – engagement etc.				

VQVC Objectives

VQVC presents another way of categorising objectives and means Volume, Quality, Value & Cost Objectives.

Volume Objectives measure: Number of unique visitors, leads, sales, active (repeat) customers.

Quality Objectives measure: Bounce rate, % conversion to lead, % conversion to sale, % conversion to active (repeat) customers

Value Objectives measure: Revenue per visit, Lifetime Value

Cost Objectives measure: Cost per visitor, Cost per lead, Cost per order, Cost per retention

See a more detailed set of objectives/metrics/measurements in appendix 6.

Marketing Objectives and Marcomms Objectives
One final point; some organizations separate marketing objectives and Marcomms objectives.

Marketing objectives are action orientated, e.g. sales, clicks and conversions, while Marcomms objectives (Marketing Communications objectives) are mentally orientated e.g. awareness, preference, positioning, and attitudes which are measured by surveys (offline or online).

2.4 Other Approaches to Setting Objectives

Let's look at some other approaches
- The Race Approach to Objectives
- The 5Ss Approach
- Inspirational Objectives

The Race Approach to Objectives
The Smart Insights RACE framework (Reach, Act, Convert and Engage) is another way of looking at objectives as the customer moves through the customer life cycle from initial contact to lifetime loyalty. Each stage can be quantified as an objective.

Reach is about increasing brand awareness to encourage visits to a website or social media, e.g. to increase new visits to your site per month by 5% or by 5,000 visitors. Act means encouraging initial interaction with content which then generates leads, e.g. to increase leads by 1% or 1,000 per month.

Convert is the ultimate conversion to sales achieved online or offline, e.g. increase online sales conversion rate by 10% from 2% to 2.2%.

Engage means post-sales engagement designed to create long term loyalty and advocacy, e.g. to generate x% engagement from existing customers or to generate x number of 5 star reviews, shares or likes.

You can see more examples of KPIs in the Control section and, in particular, where VQVC goals go beyond site visitor volume and include measures of site visit Quality, Value and Cost. This is a good example of Control/Metrics measuring performance, to inform Situation Analysis and help to refine the next set of KPI targets.

More on RACE in the Strategy section.

The 5Ss Approach to Objectives

One other, very different approach which I developed in the '90s when the internet first emerged, was 'The 5Ss': Sell, Serve, Save, Speak and Sizzle.

Sell means 'sales' targets, both online (if relevant) and offline sales influenced by online.

Serve sets customer service targets but also inspires better service (see Sizzle).

Save means to save both money and time (for both the customer and the organization) by delivering an efficient service.

Speak means conversations, listening carefully and participating. Engagement is another measure of 'speak'.

Sizzle is the digital sizzle or magic that delivers added value or digital sizzle to a brand which you simply cannot get offline.

Inspirational Objectives
All objectives, other than Sizzle, should have numbers (timescales and metrics or goals and compared to a benchmark/average). Sizzle can have numbers and certainly should be inspirational, e.g. Sir David Ramsbotham, Chief Inspector of Her Majesty's Prisons, changed the key objective from 'number of escapees' to 'number of repeat offenders'.

National Semiconductor (now owned by Texas Instruments) 'Sizzle' objective was so visionary that it created sustainable competitive advantage. 'Develop a website that wows our customers so much they'll never leave us' was the enlightened CEO's brief. See the full story in the appendices.

The Sistine Chapel in Rome Digital now has global digital sizzle so good that the website's customer experience actually beats the real-life customer experience when physically visiting the chapel.

The Virtual Sistine Chapel

The Sistine Chapel is a good example of digital sizzle. Arguably, the best website in the world with only two buttons/tabs. Yet it delivers a wonderful experience for those that want to soak it in and see it up close and uninterrupted. In fact, you can climb the walls and, if you want, stand under the great ceiling to enjoy the unique view that Michelangelo had as he stood on his giant scaffolding while painting the stunning ceiling way back in 1512. This is digital sizzle.

Visit the Vatican.VA Sistine Chapel to see Michelangelo's stunning frescos. You can move around, walk up the walls, zoom in on the ceilings and see the detail – something you simply cannot do when you visit the chapel. Don't forget to turn on your audio also.

Inspirational Objectives Include Adding Digital Sizzle
It's interesting to see how making Sizzle an objective can sometimes shake things up. 'Let's add digital Sizzle to create added value' or to 'wow' our customers or to give them a stunning customer experience. Incidentally, this can

also create competitive advantage. Here are a few summary examples:

Sistine chapel digital experience widens the reach (and interaction/experience) of visiting the Sistine chapel. Indeed, many visitors say the online experience is better than the 'real thing'.

Nike app can change a solo run into a competitive global community run with other runners across the world. Effectively, changing the customer experience from a running shoe into competing in a live global running club.

National Semiconductor, as mentioned earlier, embraced digital and created so much added digital value to their website that their customers simply cannot work without it (see appendices for more).

Technology will be at the centre of every product and service

We will soon have 'the super-efficient chips that can be empowered by ambient energy combined with cloud technology will soon put digital technology at the centre of every product and service.'
(Satell, 2012)

More and more services are converging and moving from the physical into the digital world. In fact, it is here that all products become services as added digital value services are layered onto the fundamental product.

2.5 A Sense of Purpose

Ask: 'Why does your brand matter?' If you don't know, **and** no other colleagues know, then nobody else will care. A sense of purpose at work is important – partly because customers like to buy brands that stand for something and partly because employees like to work for an organisation that stands for something more than just making money. Something deeper.

Find your sense of purpose – your mission – your passion. 'You simply cannot drive sustained performance and high levels of achievement in one's job and career without being fully engaged and feeling a strong sense of purpose. The common element that often is the spark plug for change and progress is a sense of purpose.' (Moore 2017)

'It's not about merit, professionalism, or quality. It is about faith, belief, conviction, courage, and meaning.

Because the brutal reality of today's new world is this: If you don't stand for something you're dead; it's just a question of when.' Sisodia 2014. Johnson & Johnson supports nurses while Procter & Gamble supports mums. Have you defined your organisation's purpose? World-Class **companies profit from passion and purpose.** They endear themselves to customers and communities. These companies are what Sisodia et al call **Firms of Endearment** (2014).

Firms of Endearment in 10 Years Grew Collectively at a rate of: **1000% +**	**Standard & Poor 500** in 10 Years Grew Collectively at a rate of: **122%**

"Companies who put purpose and passion at the heart of what they do are blowing away the S&P 500 averages when it comes to their performance." Sisodia et al 2014

Happiness Is A Business Model

Remember, happy employees want to create happy customers which helps to generate sales, and repeat sales, which deliver better margins, bigger profits and ultimately happy shareholders.

Happy Employees
        = Happy Customers
                = Happy Shareholders

'It's possible to "suck the fluffiness out of happiness" and make it real, measurable, and tangible' (Kuppler 2014). You must clearly define values that actually create a culture such as integrity and being innovative. Leaders encourage, and ultimately, ensure that everyone commits to this values-driven organisation in both the good times and the bad times. For example, Zappos engage their staff by asking their employees to summarise what the Zappos culture means to them. These answers are then published unedited (any typos are corrected) and published in the *Zappos Culture Book* for everyone to see.

Objectives Summary

From Mission, to Vision, to KPIs, to the 5Ss, crystal clear objectives help the organization to focus on what needs to be done. Objectives also give direction & boost motivation particularly when using 'Sizzle'.

Sensible and quantifiable objectives are easy to set once you have done a thorough Situation Analysis as you can see how you performed against the previous period's objectives. The analysis reveals strengths, weaknesses and market trends which will guide you towards making better objectives.

These objectives will be measured against the objectives that have been set (some on a daily basis and others on a quarterly basis).

The Control section also specifies what gets measured and by whom, when and, most importantly, what happens with this information – what kind of marketing decisions will be made as a result of measuring metrics.

Objectives are measured in the Control section,
which, in turn, feeds the next period's Situation Analysis.

Chapter 3 Strategy

SOSTAC® is a registered trade mark of www.PRSmith.org

Situation Analysis answers 'where are we now?'
Objectives clarify 'where do we want to go?'
and Strategy summarizes 'how do we get there?' Strategy
requires the ability to see the big picture. Strategy is, in
fact, the smallest, yet arguably the most difficult, part of a
plan. We will explore nine strategic components which
you need to consider carefully when developing your
strategy. We'll explore these in a few minutes.

Strategy harnesses capabilities
Strategy requires coherent thinking that harnesses
capabilities (existing or those that can be acquired) to
tackle problems and exploit opportunities. It is difficult to
find examples of great digital marketing strategies. Perhaps
because digital is not isolated as a digital strategy, but
rather it should be part of a broader integrated marketing
strategy.

WARNING!

'All men can see the tactics whereby I conquer,
what none can see is the strategy
out of which victory is evolved.'
Sun Tzu, The Art of War

Classic Approaches to Strategy

There are many approaches to strategy including Blue
Ocean Strategy, Porter's Competitive Advantage and
Ansoff Matrix . We'll mention them briefly. Blue Ocean
strategy avoids the 'strategic hell' of undifferentiated
products competing in price wars until someone gets

squeezed out. A Blue Ocean Strategy makes competition irrelevant and creates an uncontested market space. Apple iPhones and iPods did this. See more in Appendix 6. Porter's Strategic Competitive Advantage gives companies 3 strategic options of competing by: (1) product differentiation (includes positioning), (2) targeting niche target markets (includes targeting) or (3) competing by low cost (includes targeting and positioning). The Ansoff Matrix (p.158) looks at growth strategies derived from either choosing (a) new markets (b) existing markets (c) new products or (d) existing products d generates four strategic options for growth: (1) sell more existing product into existing markets or (2) sell more existing product into new markets or (3) sell new product into existing markets or (4) sell new products into new markets (double axes of risk!)

These are all marketing strategies that involve product decisions, in fact all of the marketing mix. We are not focussing on product portfolio strategy, but more on a digital marketing strategy for a single brand or product.

We will explore 9 Key Components which you must consider when building your digital marketing strategy. You don't have to use all 9 but at least consider all 9 components.

But first, let's start with a tragic marketing story – where the wrong marketing strategy killed a great innovation – the world's first electric-car.

3.1 Strategy – Success/Failure Difference
Lousy Marketing Strategy Kills A Great Product
This is an offline example that demonstrates two critical components that apply to every digital marketing strategy.

I hope you will see the major strategic errors before I highlight them. Once upon a time, a clever British technology inventor, Sir Clive Sinclair, created a radical innovation, the world's first electric car.He called it the Sinclair C5.

The Sinclair C5

Launched in 1985, the C5 targeted 3 groups: Women going shopping; men commuting to the station and kids playing sport during the summer. Distributed via electricity board retail stores across all UK high streets and retailing at £399. Awareness levels were extraordinarily high. Everyone knew about the C5. It needed to be charged every 70 miles and had a max speed of 30 mph. It was tested in large warehouses with simulated road experiences.

A nightmare unfolding

I wrote to Sir Clive Sinclair at Sinclair Vehicles to tell them they were making a terrible marketing strategy mistake which would destroy the innovative e-Car but which we could fix without any fee required. They wrote back to me and promised to get the marketing manager to call me. He never did, despite two calls from me.

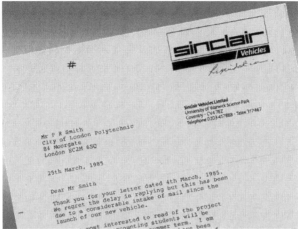

Trying to save the world's first electric car from self-destruction

The company soon went bust. The sad thing is that it could have, and should have, been a success. There was a market for this product. So, what do you think was wrong with the marketing strategy and what marketing strategy could have saved it? Stop for a moment and think.

Wrong Strategy
Firstly, positioning the C5 as a car killed it dead. Across every purchase criteria for a car (speed, safety, in-car entertainment, size etc.) it scored lowest. Secondly, targeting shoppers, commuters and kids was never going to work. There were so many other segments which could have been targeted including the greens, hot climate countries with holiday makers, or B2B markets such as airports and exhibition conference centres.

Right Strategy
When the C5 went bust, the remaining stock was liquidated and sold to a smart marketer who (a) repositioned the C5

electric car as a 'Space Rider' fun novelty item and (b) targeted at 18-35 year old holiday fun lovers in Spain. This strategic decision subsequently guided the subsequent tactical decisions regarding the marketing mix: he doubled the price, distributed C5s via moped rental shops in Spanish holiday resorts and with very simple limited promotion he sold the factory stock (at twice the purchase price) within two months. This is what he did.

Targeting and Positioning
– two major components of any marketing strategy

You can see teams of people working harder and harder, longer and longer hours, yet still failing to achieve their objectives. Why? Because, if you get the strategy wrong, the tactics will be wrong and no matter how hard you work it will just get more and more difficult to achieve your Objectives.

WARNING!

'There's no point rowing harder,
if you are rowing in the wrong direction.'

Kenichi Ohmae

In a marketing plan, or a Digital Marketing Plan, it is critical that you get these two major strategic components correct:

Target Markets means breaking markets into segments and carefully selecting the right segments to target, i.e. targeting the 'low hanging fruit'. These are the customers that you can easily reach and who really want your product or service.

Positioning means how you want to be perceived or positioned in the minds of your target market(s); ideally where there is a real customer need and little competition.

Two more recent repositioning examples are e-cigarettes and Intel. Although seemingly small and subtle changes, these are big decisions.

Positioning and targeting are so important. Consider e-cigarette company, blu-e-cig, who repositioned their e-cigarettes from:
'an alternative method to give up smoking'
to
'a lifestyle choice for smokers'

Jacob Fuller, CEO Blu-e-cig agreed and said 'Our biggest mistake was to call it an 'e-cigarette - an alternative method to give up smoking'" (Benady, 2014)

Another example of 'repositioning' is Intel, who made a bold strategic decision to change their positioning from:

'High quality technology products'
to
'Leader in technology breakthroughs'

Intel's strategy is to position itself as a leader in technology breakthroughs targeting generation Y by associating Intel with innovation in music, art and lifestyle, using social media to leverage offline real events.

This is a major strategic decision that will drive all of their tactics including: developing an online community forum called IT Galaxy; a B2B game ,outdoor 3D projections; partnering with edgy magazine 'Vice' to launch The Creators Project and Facebook app The Museum Of Me; Appointed Will.i.am, Black Eyed Peas, as director of creative innovation. Google search, TV ads, social media, PR and training (for store assistants and re-sellers).

Watch the 'Museum Of Me' video on YouTube

So, strategy drives tactics (not the other way around).

Just before we move onto the 9 components to consider in a digital marketing strategy (we've already mentioned two of them – positioning and targeting), it is worth emphasizing that positioning directly influences your Value Proposition (VP). Your VP answers your online visitor's question 'What's in it for me?' Does your website, your content and your social media platforms all express a clear and immediate VP?

3.2 Positioning and Your Value Proposition

A company website offers great opportunities to offer added value to the customer experience which simply isn't available offline. This added value can vary from new types of content to entertain or to inform (e.g. how to use your products), to new types of interactive services like a customer community or some 'sizzle' like the Sistine Chapel digital experience (mentioned in the Objectives section). Many businesses miss out on the opportunity of adding digital value to physical products and services (not just online products and services).

Value Proposition

A   value proposition (VP) is closely tied to your brand's positioning which answers questions such as: Who are we? What do we offer? Which markets do we serve? What makes us different? And the customer's crunch question: What's in it for me? which needs to be answered within seconds of landing on a website.

VP is more than just selling

Your VP is more than just a selling proposition since it shows what you can offer by way of content, products, services and experiences to engage online customers. The VP extends this difference in that it identifies the reasons why customers will click on, return to, register or buy from your site and, ideally, feel motivated enough to share their experience.

 VP – part of ongoing integrated communications
Your VP should be developed around your audience personas, support commercial goals and be communicated as part of ongoing integrated communications to encourage prospects to experience this value. The VP can only be developed after the positioning has been decided.

Targeting and Positioning are just two of the 9 key components of digital marketing strategy. Let's explore all 9 now.

3.3 Components of Digital Marketing Strategy

TOPPP SEED (9 Key Components)
Here are 9 key components to consider when building your digital marketing strategy. You do not have to use all 9 key components in your digital marketing strategy. In fact, the strategy excerpts I'll show you later only include a selection of these 9 key components. You may find some components overlap/integrate. This is good. Your strategy doesn't have to be in the same order as TOPPP SEED. Feel free to move the components around to suit your strategy. Now let's consider each of the 9 components to help you to build a crystal clear digital marketing strategy.

- Target Markets (essential)
- Objectives (it's helpful to summarize what objectives the strategy will fulfil)
- Positioning (essential)

- Processes (new processes like a new CRM system or a new marketing automation system or AI)
- Partnership (strategic alliances, co-marketing or marketing marriages can make marketing more cost effective)
- Sequence (or stages, e.g. Develop Credibility before Raising Visibility)
- Experience (The Customer Experience or 'CX' are you creating a new CX or a different CX?)
- Engagement (what level of the Ladder of Customer Engagement is required?)
- Data (can data be used to add value, or target new customers – this may overlap with 'Processes' – major opportunity here)

Let's take a look at each of these briefly.

3.3.1 TARGET MARKETS

Target markets need to be defined very clearly. Today we have many new variables (or filters) to help marketers identify targets. Time and effort spent carefully analyzing and discussing who is/are the most ideal target market/s is time well spent. The more detailed target customer profiles, the easier it is to find the customers.

After profiling the target markets, we then describe several types of personae which helps copywriters, designers and all marketers deliver much better communications (see p.

Two alternative targeting strategies might be: (1) Cast a wide net and target a large group of prospects or (2) Target a much smaller niche with tailored offerings.

In B2B marketing this is becoming more popular, in particular. They call it **Account Based Marketing** (ABM) which targets a defined set of target clients (prospects or accounts) and then designs personalized/tailored campaigns that resonate with each prospect's particular needs. Don't forget to create personas (see appendices).

3.3.2 OBJECTIVES

It is always worth double checking that your strategy actually supports the 'big' objectives (Mission and Vision) as well as the target sales, market share and ROI. Strategy without reference to objectives is unlikely to achieve those objectives. Hence some organizations want to see the main objectives referred to when presenting their strategies.

Deciding which is a priority objective - Customer Acquisition or Customer Retention or, alternatively, creating new products targeted at either (a) the same market or (b) a new market, are all strategic growth options. Igor Ansoff developed his matrix way back in the 1950s. Today it helps generate strategic growth options. Here's Ansoff strategic growth options applied to Netflix.

		Market Penetration	Market Development
P R O D U C T S	Existing		
	New		
		Product Development	Diversification
		Existing	New

MARKETS

Netflix could have chosen to stay in the DVD market and seek growth through market penetration (getting more market share/market penetration). Alternatively, they could target new markets around the world – albeit all these options are in shrinking markets.

Instead, a Product Development option, Movie Streaming, was chosen. More recently Netflix are exploring New Products in New Markets (ie diversification which includes vertical growth (moving up and down the supply chain) – Netflix Cinemas and Netflix film productions – both of which can be categorised as diversification (if you define their original product as DVDs and not just broader 'entertainment'.

1. DVDS in USA
2. DVDS Worldwide
3. Movie Streaming USA
4. Movie Streaming Worldwide
5. Cinemas USA
6. Movie Production

All strategic options (1-6 and more) are analysed carefully. The pro's (demand growth, profit margins etc.) and cons (competition, low barriers to entry etc.) are scored, weighted and added up.

Other variables like strategic fit (does it fit with (a) the organisation's Mission and (b) an unstoppable market trend) are also calculated, scored and weighted to help make a final strategic choice.

3.3.3 POSITIONING

Positioning is so strategic that you really don't want to be changing this each year. Positioning means precisely how you want to be positioned (or perceived) in the minds of your target customers. Note: Positioning is the foundation for brand propositions (what's in it for the customer) and ultimately, the customer experience (CX). In fact, defining the brand, the VP and the CX are part of strategy. VP and CX also influence the subsequent marketing mix decisions (tactical decisions), e.g. exclusive products online; differential pricing; exclusive online promotions; prioritizing which channels; online distribution partners etc. See 'Tactics' for more.

The Classic Repositioning Case:
from Sick Child to Healthy Adult

Lucozade repositioned itself from a 'sick child's drink' to a 'healthy adult's drink'. They followed the market trends: the demographic shift from a massive child market (baby boom) in the 1960s to a bulging 40 year old market in the noughties (2000s). They also followed the trend towards 'healthy living'. This repositioning strategy drives changes across all of the marketing mix tactics from chemist shop distribution and 'mother and child' ads to sports celebrity ads and Coca-Cola style distribution into shops, restaurants and offices.

3.3.4 PROCESSES

If you are introducing a new approach, a new process, a system or even new way of thinking, this can be strategic, e.g. introducing Marketing Automation or adding AI chat bots to your customer service channels or working with new IoT partners or insisting on analytics driven decisions, or, nurturing a 'Constant Beta Culture' (constant A/B testing / optimization of web pages, emails, and ads), or, integrating all data from all touchpoints to generate a real-time (immediately updated) 360 degree customer view to facilitate a personalized and tailored Customer Experience.

These are significantly new processes which will disrupt staff, departments and organization structures. Hence these are new processes, when introduced are definitely a strategic issue.

WARNING!

Most of these new processes fail! E.g. over 50% of new CRM systems fail. See the Action Section which explains why they fail and how to ensure your processes never fail.

Processes are important. The idea of introducing new processes can be considered strategic. Processes also appear in the 'Tactics' section (what happens when) and the finer, working details (that ensure processes are actually executed properly) such as checklists, training, motivation and communication are specified in the 'Action' section of the plan (e.g. the detailed process of producing world class Marketing Content).

Processes such as programmatic ads, AI personalization and marketing automation are also referred to in another strategic component: 'Sequence' section.

Finally, major new processes will probably require re-allocating your team to some different jobs. Do you need a new marketing team structure or employ external agencies to manage the process of marketing? Either way, internal marketing (communication, motivation and training) will be required. See 'Actions' section for more on internal marketing.

3.3.5 PARTNERSHIPS (and collaborations)

Partnership – introducing, strengthening or reducing strategic partnership/marketing marriages/marketing alliances is part of strategy. Are there partners out there that can extend (a) your reach or (b) your product portfolio?

Are there potential partners out there whose customers would welcome your organization's products or services (including your content marketing?

Partnership Strategy Worked For Amazon

...the dot-com bubble hit Amazon in year 2000. Stock price crashed to $5.97 per share. It seemed like the end for Amazon due to extremely low investor confidence in online marketplace model.

Bezos did not give up. He saw the big picture of making Amazon the world's largest retailer and stuck to it. Innovation, again was the key. In order to grow the customer base it was necessary to garner greater traction on its online presence through collaboration with physical stores. Thus it partnered with Target, Toys-R-Us, GAP and 400 other retailers for expanding its reach. Amazon was back in the picture again and it has never looked back since.
Soumya 2017

Note: Amazon also purchased key online publishers like (IMDB.com to market its DVDs and DPReview.com to encourage purchase of cameras from Amazon by people comparing cameras).

IoT – New Partnerships Opportunity

IoT also offers many new partnership opportunities. Are there new, emerging, potential IoT partners out there whose products (or network of interconnected devices) could deliver your products and services (&/or your marketing content) in a new and exciting way to an audience that fits your ideal customer profile?

Selecting the right partner can firstly give you access to a much bigger target market and secondly, strengthen your brand. But remember partnerships have to benefit both parties, with clear goals, roles and responsibilities – 'the devil is, most definitely, in the detail'.

#alwayson Smart Bags 'Surprise & Delight'

Rebecca Minkoff luxury handbags and accessories have joined the growing Internet of Things (IoT) movement in retail. The brand's #alwayson bags have a code which, when scanned via smartphone, will let the bag owners receive 'surprise & delight' product recommendations, exclusive offers, and video content from Rebecca Minkoff. Olsen 2017

IoT Driven by EVRYTHNG

The value exchange is clear: Consumers get personalized experiences after scanning their bag, and the brand acquire new, direct customer relationships (& data).

Leveraging Digital Emotional Intelligence
Unlocking the power of personalization. Put simply, it means brands can get to know consumers better, amplifying and responding to their emotions.

In turn, consumers feel more connected to the brand and feel a greater affinity. Perrin 2017

3.3.6 SEQUENCE or STAGES

Develop credibility before raising visibility. How many businesses get that one wrong? How many major TV ad campaigns or content marketing and social media platforms drive traffic to websites or apps that don't work?

Develop Credibility Before Raising Visibility
It is so important that I thought I'd mention it again!

AIDA (Attention/Awareness, Interest, Desire & Action /Buy). There are many variations of this 100 year old model. Regardless, you have to build awareness and Trust before you can build brand preference and certainly before you can seek sales . So building awareness and preference might be phase 1 and converting this to sales could be stage 2 (customer acquisition) , and stage 3 customer retention (more on this later). .

Diffusion of Innovations - surprisingly, markets still follow Rogers classic 'Diffusion of Innovations' pattern. So, if you have a genuine innovation, there are 5 different segments of customers, including the Innovators & Early Adopters who are risk seekers and embrace innovation, while the Early Majority will wait until the Innovators and Early Adopters have started buying. Late Majority follow and the 'Laggards' who are risk averse and avoid innovation at all costs. before roll-out

RACE - another approach is Dave Chaffey's RACE Reach means increasing awareness and encouraging visits; Act means initial interaction; Convert means conversion to sales; Engage means post-sales engagement designed to create long term loyalty and advocacy.

TOFU MOFU BOFU

More acronyms – these refer to the sales funnel we discussed in the Objectives section)
TOFU means Top Of sales FUnnel (awareness)
MOFU equals Middle Of FUnnel (interest/desire)
BOFU – Bottom Of the FUnnel (action/buy stage)

Customer Acquisition v Customer Retention

Obviously, retention can only come after acquisition. However, you still need to plan for retention. In year 2, perhaps you might spend more on Stage 2: Retention (than you previously spent on Stage 1: Acquisition)?

You must decide which has priority: Acquisition or Retention (and then determine what resources will be allocated to each). You have to acquire customers before you can retain them. But once you have acquired customers, shouldn't you focus on stage 2 i.e. Customer Retention which is deemed to be, on average, six times more profitable than customer acquisition. Therefore, plan for customer retention communications once customers are acquired. This requires a strategic shift in thinking. See the Tactics section for three stunning tactical approaches to retaining customers (involving ads, sales promotions and CSR).

Flexible Common Sense Sequence or Resequencing

During major breaking news events, Mailchimp turn off all promoted and scheduled social posts. Mailchimp

---

Long Term Life Time v Short Term Transactional

In essence, strategy should have more of a long-term perspective while tactics are more short term. The long-term view introduces lifetime customers and lifetime customer experience (which has many stages). This type of thinking changes everything and ensures a more strategic approach.

> ## Map out the customer lifecycle journey...
>
> ... and then deploy processes such as automated, always-on communications like Programmatic Ads to build awareness, AI-based Personalisation to improve conversions and marketing automation to nurture customer relations by delivering more relevant messages via email, app and web site.
> Adapted from Dave Chaffey

Always-On Campaigns

This brings us to 'Always-On communications sequence' driven by marketing automation so that the customer is continually helped through every step of the ongoing Customer Lifetime Journey. This 'Always On' approach helps management by defining what content is served to whom at every stage of the journey (before, during and after each purchase). So whether the management schedule series of emails, texts or social media announcements and paid media activities, or deliver marketing content triggered by individual customer click behaviour, the net result is continual conversation 24/7/365.

> ## The Cruel Sound Of Silence
>
> One cruel form of punishment in prisons is the silence in solitary confinement. So why do some of our high profile brands go silent on us - instead of being 'Always On'?

3.3.7 ENGAGEMENT

There are different levels of visitor engagement. From encouraging visitors and customers to give ratings and reviews to nurturing advocates to collaborating and co-creating ideas and products.

This is the Ladder Of Engagement starting with low level engagement (ratings and reviews) and at the top of the ladder is collaborative co-creation.

The Ladder Of Engagement from Marketing Communications 7th ed Smith and Zook (2020)

But also remember that not everyone wants to engage all the time, sometimes visitors just want to complete a task, find some information or just buy something and leave your site. So, don't ignore the basics of properly tested, quick, easy-to-use websites and apps.

3.3.8 EXPERIENCE (the Customer Experience / CX)

Defining what kind of customer experience you want your customers to have is at the heart of your business and your strategy. Personalized, real-time, fast and efficient or fun, relaxing and enjoyable?

Costco v Apple Customer Experience (CX)

Costco customers expect bare-bones service in return for low prices, while Apple customers expect high quality innovative products at relatively high prices. Those are very different customer experiences, but they both delight customers (Brand & Hagen, 2011). And they are delivered to customers consistently online and offline.

What a brand says about itself (through its brand positioning and brand propositions) is less important than the actual experience the brand delivers to its customers across all touch-points. So, although positioning and brand propositions are important they are less important than the actual customers' experiences (CX).

The CX establishes the brand experience which needs to be clearly defined:

- Is the CX you are defining a 'one-off CX' or a 'Lifetime CX?'. Next question, ask yourself:
- Can you deliver the perfect 'Lifetime CX'?
- What is the perfect Lifetime CX? Describe it.
- Can AI help your CX?
- Also can the CX should be personalized and available in real time i.e. whenever the customer

wants it, or exactly when would the customer really appreciate being offered your product/service or content?

The CX needs to be managed across functions, by all staff online and offline. So, Positioning drives propositions which influence the CX.

Some marketers define the CX along with the positioning and propositions. Others define them separately at the end and add them to their strategy.

IoT can Add Value to the CX

'Smart, connected products raise a new set of strategic choices related to 'how value is captured' and delivered. IoT presents an opportunity for all products to add extra value to help customers in new ways. IoT also delivers a new threat from a new era of competitors who are disrupting the old value chains. Harvard's Porter & Hepplemann (2014)

IoT Affects CX
The Internet of Things (IoT) connects products with data and even other products (and services) via chips, sensors, software, networks, and partners in a myriad of new and exciting ways that boost customer experiences and change the nature of your business in a radically new way.

IoT CX Examples
Tennis rackets containing sensors and connectivity in the racket handle allows manufacturers* to help players improve their game through the tracking and analysis of ball speed, spin, and impact location - all delivered via a smartphone application (* Babolat Play Pure Drive).

A second example is Whirlpool, a leader in the connected home, which 'includes connected appliances including automated lighting, HVAC, entertainment, and security.

This is now a product-as-a-service since Whirlpool maintains ownership of the product and the customer simply pays for the use of the machine'. Porter & Hepplemann (2014)

Reinventing The Entire Arc Of The CX

..helped Zipcar to turn car-sharing into a mainstream business, and do environmental good at the same time.
For Zipcar, the experience begins on the website for both prospective and existing customers. People can find out about the service, sign up as members, find and reserve nearby cars, and manage their accounts. All aspects of being a Zipcar member have been thought through, from which cars to have in the fleet to how people identify which car is theirs to use at a given time; from handling gas station stops to insurance of the car and passengers; from parking space location to fleet management.

Richardson 2010

Content Marketing
– a growing part of the Customer Experience
If say, more than 85% of Google searches are for useful information and only 10% of searches are for products and services , it follows that producing good quality content will satisfy searchers' needs and give them a good experience.

It also satisfies Googles criteria for SEO which is basically relevant high-quality content that people like (and engage with) across multiple platforms (don't forget to put high quality content on your homepage too).

You will see that Content Marketing is listed amongst 10 other tactical tools (in the Tactics section) but should it be number one? Well, for companies like Red Bull, it is. It is the driving force behind their marketing strategy.

Some companies keep it simple, like Red Bull, and spend most of their money on content that their demographic really wants.

Red Bull recently released an 81minute movie 'Where the Trail Ends' - this was after they had sponsored Red Bull Stratos - Mission to the Edge of Space and Supersonic Freefall parachute jump, which was made into a TV documentary complete with photo gallery and video gallery and media tour. Red Bull content is simply excellent.

Red Bull's contents support what their customers want and also the brand values. Source: Red Bull.

Can you deliver a stream of relevant added-value content that your customers will appreciate? Can you do this better than competition? Can you deliver it in real-time – just when they need it (just when their digital body language indicates they are ready for this content)?

So, it is worth considering whether content marketing could be the lead component in your digital marketing strategy, but remember it's competitive out there and there's a lot of other content competing for your customers' shortened attention spans. See p.219 for more on Content Marketing.

3.3.9 DATA

...the last of the TOPPP SEED components of strategy yet some would say that it is the most important component ..... remember TOPPP SEED is not in any order of importance... it just an acronym to help you think about various aspects of strategy.

Integrating customer data online and offline is a strategic decision. From click behaviour data (digital body language), to registration data, to social media data to CRM (Customer Relationship Management) to purchase behaviour, to post-purchase contact data (including complaints).

After that you can layer it with external data from third party databases. 'Having social data as well as a complete history of your leads' and customers' activity in one place is invaluable to your company, because it means you can finally stop wasting time on what doesn't work, as well as equipping your sales team with the information to help them close more deals.' (Toner, 2014)

You must give an **integrated 360 customer view** (that brings together each customer's data from online (web sites, apps, social media etc.) and offline platforms (telephone, in-store etc.).

This means that **all the processes (already discussed) must be integrated** so data can flow between them to ensure a single 360 view of the customer.

Data can be used to personalise the CX in real-time so that we can help customers with exactly what they need, when they need it.

Learn to ask questions of your data.

Three Great Data Questions

1. Can you integrate your data?

2. How can data add value to the Perfect Lifetime CX – to help customers to 'get the job done'?

3. Can you use your data to profile and target customers with more relevant offers, just when they need it?

Data Sharing & IoT
It's a strategic decision to integrate data, or even just embed chips and sharing data between different companies

or partners (e.g. Whirlpool) to deliver new benefits to customers. So IoT also requires strategic partnerships.

WARNING!

Bad or Incomplete or Unintegrated Data Damages Your Business

'Data is the world's most valuable resource.' But equally bad or incomplete data can damage your brand permanently. Late data, unintegrated data, repeat data requests, incomplete customer data e.g .they complained via twitter but no one in the sales department knows that this customer is unhappy. So develop an interest in the <u>many different digital marketing tools</u> and how they integrate data.

Summary TOPPP SEED Components & IoT

Using the TOPPP SEED strategic components (Target Markets, Objectives, Positioning, Partners, Processes, Sequence, Engagement , Experience and Data), we can see IoT is part of both Partnerships and Data Integration. IoT requires new Partners since IoT offers major opportunities to create added value by connecting to or sharing a partner's product/services' benefits with existing customers. IoT definitely requires data to be integrated from offline to online and also from one product or service to another and from one partner to another (as long as there are no breaches of data protection and privacy).

This IoT section is taken from a 2016 PR Smith blog post entitled 'IoT Is Here' on prsmith.org/blog For more on this see the appendices, the reference and the blog post.

Boardroom Tip – watch the cash

Be clear about exactly how much resource your strategy requires. Your board will want to know exactly what budget and people resources are required. Budgets don't always have to be included in a strategy, however mentioning budget, or 'spend' keeps your presentation very grounded, i.e. forces marketers to at least announce what resources are required to deliver this strategy.

3.4 Sample Strategy Excerpts

Here is a selection of excerpts from digital marketing strategies. See if you can identify which strategic components from TOPPP SEED are being used:

Target markets; Objectives; Positioning; Partnerships; Processes; Sequence/Stages; Engagement; Experience (CX); Data.

When you bring several, if not all, of these 9 components together, the digital marketing strategy moves closer to a business strategy. e.g. just positioning, partners and data components can redefine a business.

Strategy Excerpt	TOPPP SEED Component
	Target markets; Objectives;

	Positioning; Partnerships;Processes; Sequence/Stages; Engagement Level; Experience (CX); Data
Uber Uber's clever algorithms use data and devices to create a service (product) that improves the CX by reducing the customer's cognitive load', reducing prices and reducing waiting time for any customer who needs a taxi, all done via a clever app. Uber wants to be seen (positioned) as a 'personal drive from any point at any time' (for customers) and also a 'business/hobby driving people for money' (for drivers). For governments Uber wanted to be seen as a data company rather than a transport company (however, the EU has ruled it is a transport company). Uber growth strategy via to: (a) get new customers and (b) enter new markets.	Data Experience Positioning Target Mkts Sequence (new customers..)
Amazon Amazon's ever-expanding product portfolio, combined with low pricing, world's best processes, data-driven personalised offers and ever-growing distribution partnerships has, in fact, defined its overall business strategy. Some describe it as 'cost leadership taken to the extreme.' The global online retailer 'operates with a razor thin profit margin and succeeds due to a combination of economies of scale, innovation of various business processes and a constant business diversification. Amazon	Positioning (wide product offering & low priced) Data Experience (customer focus) Sequence (long term)

business strategy is guided by four principles: customer obsession rather than competitor focus, passion for invention, commitment to operational excellence, and long-term thinking.'	
Facebook (in specific developing countries) Position fb as 'The Internet' ...Key to Facebook's strategy is ...no matter where users start on the ladder of mobile technology, (from the most basic device to the newest smartphone), Facebook (which starts free) becomes better and more fun to use as they upgrade.	Positioning Targeting Engagement ...
HSBAC Drive carefully targeted prospect traffic via a blend of inbound and outbound marketing using Marketing Automation and subsequently building incremental profiling via data profiling to ensure added value relevant offers and timely advice – reassure and reinvigorate customer relationships.	Target Mkt. Data Process (Mktg Automation) Sequence ...
Paypal A two phased Automated Email campaign supported by banner ads and telemarketing and a 'fully mobile optimized' microsite using high quality content that not only helped merchants to	Process (MA) Sequence (Banner & Telemktg) Tools (email, telemarketing

understand the mobile opportunity, but which also helped them to begin their own mobilization process.	Experience (microsite & content marketing)....
RABODirect Grow fan base by engaging fans via social engagement through the development of a dynamic Twitter engagement tool called RaboScore complete with a leaderboard ranking the top 12 fans of the competition and use Gamification and online rewards to continually drive engagement, particularly with key online influencers.	Targeting Engagement Sequence ...
FT Become a 'data asset driven business' positioning FT global business news niche with unique content targeting the moneying classes offering a flexible (multiple niching) product & flexible pricing (product can be mixed and matched into all kinds of recipes — metro, regional, or local; daily or weekly; newspaper or magazine) targeting primary B2B companies and education institutes via direct sales (rather than aggregators like Lexis Nexis and News Corp.'s Factiva) and also nurturing from registration mid funnel prospects to subscribers.	Positioning Targeting Partners Data ...

3.5 Your Strategy Template

Now use this TOPPP SEED Strategy Template. Fill in and use whichever bits in whatever order feels right – delete the rest.

To achieve
.... sales
(Objectives)
from ....(how many?) customers generating
............% market share from by................(when)

by Targeting (target markets and personas)
....,

Positioned as
.... (crystal
clear positioning)
delivering ....(what
kind of an Experience/customer experience)
over .... (how many Stages
programme e.g. gaining endorsement from influencers;
generating awareness initially followed by sales)
using any Content Marketing – some strategies are built
around Content Marketing)

and Partnering with... (are
there any strategic partners that help you extend your reach
or add value to your proposition?)

and using/integrating customer Data ....
(t profile and target customers with more relevant/tailored
offerings)

Using..(
any new Processes, e.g. marketing automation,   to CRM
wrapping an automated and personalized contact 'strategy'
around the customer lifetime journey…..).

To Engage
....(prospects,
customers and advocates)
at... (specify which
level of engagement [low level: liking/sharing, ratings,
reviews and discussions or collaborative co-creation] crowd
sourcing ideas)..

Requiring a budget (Spend) of................... (increasing or
reducing in stages 1,2,and 3) and with a team of............

When you have written your first digital marketing strategy
you will feel a little uncomfortable with it as it may well be
your first time writing a digital marketing strategy. It does
get easier. Basically, you've now got some of the key
components. You don't need to use them all, but do at least,
consider each component to see if it can help to improve
your strategy. Does it improve the big picture? Does it give
clear direction and help to guide the selection of tactical
tools?

Now rewrite your draft strategy (from the template) onto a
blank piece of paper. Change the order or format – once
you've considered all 9 components use as many as you
feel relevant and rewrite your strategy in your own words.

Then try to develop a second strategic option. A different
strategy. There is more than one way to achieve the

objectives. Some ways are better than others. You'll start to see this as you develop other alternative strategic options. Try to do this before selecting the best strategy. When you have your best strategy, you can use this next checklist to double check how good is your strategy.

Boardroom Tip
big strategic challenge is change management

Getting your own business to buy into your strategy can sometimes prove too difficult. Given that many, if not most, companies are dysfunctional and siloed to a greater or lesser degree, winning the business over to your new strategy (and getting them to understand it) is often a very challenging task, particularly if you are introducing some innovative ideas like combining your new 'content marketing' strategy with a new marketing automation process.

Many of us have a neurotic resistance to change. So rehearse the logic of your new strategy and prepare for the typical Q and A that will follow your presentation.

Do not take the criticism personally, it can be healthy and force you to check the robustness of your strategy.

3.6 Your Strategy Questions

Be ready, your board might ask you:	Yes/No
Does your strategy seize opportunities to help customers even better via digital?'	
Does your strategy clearly address 'What Problem Am I Trying To Solve?' and then see if your strategy solves it.	
Does your strategy improve the customer experience?	
Does your strategy build relationships with customers?	
Does your strategy strengthen your brand(s)?	
Does it create competitive advantage?	
Does it move with market trends?	
Are mobile, content marketing and social media part of your strategy?	
Do you have, or can you get, the resources required?	
Have you considered several strategic options before choosing this strategy?	

WARNING!

'Culture eats strategy for breakfast'

Peter Drucker once said this. You need to ensure your team actually buys into your wonderful strategy. To do this you need to spend resources on internal marketing (see 'Action' section).

However, it's worth remembering that digital is only part of any solution/strategy since it is still 'people' who execute a strategy.

See the Action section to discover how Action can help to execute tactics – the details of strategy. For now, however, let's move on and consider Tactics (or tactical tools).

**'Strategy without tactics
is the slowest route to victory'**
Sun Tzu, The Art of War

Chapter 4 Tactics

SOSTAC® is a registered trade mark of www.PRSmith.org

While strategy paints the bigger picture and ensures everything moves in the right direction, tactics are simply the details of strategy (i.e. the marketing mix).

WARNING!

'Tactics without strategy is the noise before defeat.'
Sun Tzu, The Art of War

Tactical decisions are driven by the overarching strategy. A crystal-clear positioning statement makes tactical decisions much easier. As does clearly defined target markets and what you are trying to achieve with them (objectives).

The traditional marketing mix covers decisions marketers have to make about: Product, Price, Place, Promotion, Physical Evidence, Processes and People. NB 'Processes' here refer to the operational process of creating and delivering a service (e.g. a meal or a flight) and not marketing processes which were discussed in the strategy section.

Your Tactics section in your plan has to specify your product range your prices need to specify whether they are premium prices or cut-price (and whether they dynamically change according to click behaviour location, weather, or in the case of Uber, 'the economics of supply and demand at a particular time in a particular area. etc.), plus whether you will also price (and accept payment) in digital currencies such as bit coin; 'Place' reminds marketers to specify which channels you are using to help customers to buy your products go to market (these can overlap directly with promotional channels).

Tactics gets down into the nitty gritty of which tactical promotional tools (the communications mix) will be used when, to achieve what and with how much budget as the customers move through the customer lifetime experience.

4.1 Digital Tactics Morph Marketing Mix

Digital blurs the lines of the traditional marketing mix (e.g. social media is part of the product/ experience, the promotional reach, the physical evidence, and also place/distribution).
Content Marketing is part of the product experience/customer experience (CX) plus it is also a promotional tool (usually part of sales promotion i.e. signup and you can download the content). A single decision can affect several elements of the old marketing mix.

Consider also 'Location Marketing'. It identifies customers with mobile phones in specific places and then offers special prices and promotions.
Dynamic pricing (determined by your second visit to buy an airline ticket or by your location).

So therefore, let's focus on the Communications Mix (also known as the Promotional Mix which, is one of the original '4Ps' in the Marketing Mix) while acknowledging that detailed decisions about prices, product lines and distribution channels have to also be carefully considered.

Having said all that, a clear overarching digital marketing strategy guides these detailed tactical decisions.

4.2 Ten Tactical Tools (The Communications Mix)

Advertising	Google Ads - Display Network Google Ads - Search Google Ads - Remarketing Google Ads - Customer Match Facebook - Awareness Facebook - Retargeting LinkedIn etc. Programmatic
Public Relations	Online editorial, newsletters, ezines, discussion groups, viral marketing, vine
Sponsorship	Sponsoring online events/sites service
Sales Force/ Agents/Tele-marketing	Virtual sales staff, affiliate marketing, web rings, links/chat
Exhibitions, Events and Conferences	Virtual exhibitions, virtual events, webinars
Direct Mail	Opt-in email and eNewsletter
Retail Store or Office HQ	Website (SEO and marketing automation opportunity)

Word Of Mouth	Recommendations, criticisms, feedback devices (e.g. reevoo.com), social media platforms, forums
Sales Promotion	Content Marketing, incentives, rewards, online loyalty schemes, competitions
Merchandising and Packaging	e-tailing, QR Codes, augmented reality, virtual reality. NB real packaging must be displayed online

4.3 Tactics - Help Customers Move Through Their Lifetime Journey

There are exceptions to these generalizations, e.g. as well as building awareness, advertising can build positive attitudes and preference and even nudge people into buying (particularly remarketing and retargeting ads); Exhibitions can help to establish a presence (or build awareness – 'we have to be there since competition is there'), however I argue that there may be more cost-effective ways to build awareness.

Hence, I've simplified the purpose or objectives of each tactical tool as customers move through their lifetime journey. At the very least the table (on the next page) may generate a discussion regarding which tools will do what for your organization.

The MarComms Mix: 10 Tactical Tools	Primary Purpose / Objective
Advertising	Awareness (and credibility) plus with retargeting/ remarketing triggers action
Public Relations	Awareness (and credibility/reputation)
Sponsorship	Awareness (and credibility and sampling)
Sales Force/ Agents/Telemarketing	Sales (and relationship building and gathering information)
Exhibitions, Events and Conferences	Sales (and relationship building and gathering information)
Direct Mail	Sales (and relationship building and database cleaning)
Retail Store /Office HQ/Hub/Website	Relationship building, database building, identifying prospects, enquiries, sales and CRM
Word Of Mouth	Awareness, Credibility (including endorsements and recommendations),
Sales Promotion	Converting prospects into customers (enquiry/ lead/ newsletter/ sale, post-sale relationship)
Merchandising and Packaging	Conversion and relationship building

The purpose/objectives (in the previous table) are somewhat oversimplified. E.g. Advertising is used to build awareness. It can also be used to reassure existing buyers that they are buying the right brands in the case of car advertisements. PPC ads (and even display ads) can also arouse sufficient interest that a percentage of the audience will click through to a website or a social media platform to eventually convert (whether this is registering for a newsletter, making an enquiry, trying a sample, buying a product or engaging with content that strengthens the ongoing relationships).

Gamification – Sales Promotion - Tactics

Is gamification a tactical tool? I tend to categories it as a sales promotion (and therefore a tactical tool) whether it is aimed at customers, employees, distributors or any other stakeholder. See Gamification The Good , The Bad and The Ugly (on prsmith.org/blog for more).

Real Time Marketing – Strategy or Tactics?

'Real Time Marketing' is by some, considered a strategic decision that eventually cascades down into the tactics. There are several interpretations including:

- Quick release/reaction marketing to external current events and cultural happenings – usually ads.

- Quick release/reaction marketing that finds a way to inject its brand as relevant in a conversation – social media news-jacking.

- Marketing that automatically delivers dynamic, personalized content across multi-channels (marketing automation) triggered by click behaviour, purchase behaviour, a buyer's buying cycle, or a sequence of contacts (including email).

4.4 Which Communications Tactics Should You Use?

One of the big decisions, 'which tactical tools to use' is partially answered by the objectives already set. Building awareness is often best done by advertising, PR and Sponsorship, while converting awareness, or ideally preference, into sales can require direct mail (email and/or snail mail), websites (with strong calls to action) and/or sales people (face to face, online or virtual) in retail stories, on the street or at events.

Each of these tools should be supported with some relevant sales promotion whether this is a gift or some useful marketing content to help to convert the prospect to the next stage. Again, there are, of course, exceptions.

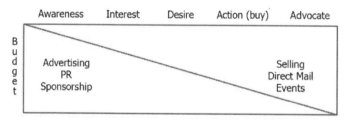

Splitting the marketing budget depending on what your objective is
e.g. awareness or selling (B2C)

The future of any organization depends on repeat business ie keeping customers for life, let's move from a one-off transactional approach (above) to thinking about which tactical tools work best throughout the customers' journey.

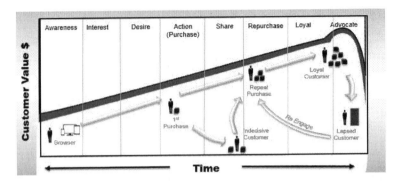

The customer lifetime experience (adapted from Dave Chaffey)

In general, if you need to build awareness you spend more on ads, PR and sponsorship. If you already have awareness, you can convert this into preference and eventually sales by increasing expenditure on selling (including chat bots), direct mail (and email), events, conferences and exhibitions. There are exceptions. Some ads (remarketing) are designed to sell directly, or at least drive traffic to a website or even to a telemarketing team (or soon a chatbot team) that will complete the sale.

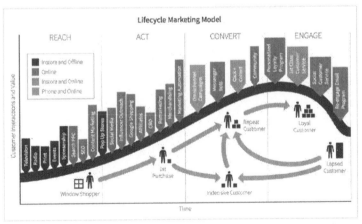

Lifecycle Marketing: Tactical Options (Dave Chaffey's Smart Insights)

Customer Retention Tactics
v Customer Acquisition Tactics
Your digital marketing strategy will have identified which
has priority: Customer Acquisition or Customer Retention
(and therefore determine what resources will be allocated to
each).

A customer's LTV (Life Time Value) might be worth sales
of say, 20 cars or 50 mobile phones (during the customer's
life). Obviously, this is worth a lot more than selling one
car or one mobile and, hence, why customer retention is
deemed to be, on average, 6 times more profitable than
customer acquisition. It is therefore, generally speaking,
worth investing in customer retention.

Let's assume you have identified retention as part of the
strategy. Once a company embraces this idea the culture
becomes more customer-centric, and part of this is
carefully anticipating and planning when a customer is due
to move back into the repeat buying cycle, so marketers can
optimize their offers at precisely the right time and block
out competition with timely and relevant service.

Customer Retention Tactics That 'Wow'
Here are three stunning customer retention examples using
different tactics from sales promotions, to ads, to CSR
(Corporate Social Responsibility Programmes) – all three
also integrate with social media tactics. Sit back and enjoy
these amazing tactical approaches to taking care of your
existing customers (and getting some publicity for it).

1. Ulster Rugby
Rewards some customers for renewing their season tickets
by giving them the very personal touch (a beautiful
customer experience) which makes great social media

content, which in turn spreads awareness, affection, liking and maybe further down the road opens up the opportunity to convert some more sales. Here's Some 'Wow' Customer Retention! (see the video, and post, about customer retention at prsmith.org/blog).

Customer Retention Isn't Boring with Ulster Rugby
– watch this video on prsmith.org/blog

2. Sports Club Recife
Now this is a truly unique approach to customer retention by Brazilian football club Sport Club Recife who reinforced their club's community feeling by launching an organ donor campaign. A CSR programme (Corporate Social Responsibility) programme. It strengthens the real community feeling that fans experience when they follow a club passionately. Driven by the club's Facebook page, some leaflets and posters, the club now has 51,000 donors (the stadium only holds 41,000) with waiting lists for hearts, lungs and eyes eradicated. See how excited the fans are about this CSR programme.

See this stunning video 'Wow Customer Retention' on prsmith.org/blog

3. TD Bank

TD bank in Canada turned ATMs into Automated Thanking Machines™ to create some very special moments for customers across the country. A simple thank you can change someone's day. #TDThanksYou adds a personalized gift to it and people get very happy.

This is 'psychic income', e.g. two tickets to a baseball game cost, say, $90. If you give someone $90 cash it won't be remembered as much as two tickets to see a baseball game. Why? Because this addresses Maslow's higher-level needs – transcendental/self-actualization. Add a relevant gift and people get ecstatic. See TD's Automated Thanking Machine™. It wows customers.

See this TD emotional video in 'Wow Customer Retention' on prsmith.org/blog

In each case the organization owns the media (the video) and they can post it on their 'owned channels', i.e. on their own YouTube channel, Facebook, Google+, Twitter stream, website and other social media platforms. This is 'owned media'. If they decide to 'promote' a post or a tweet, this is 'paid media' as is any form of 'sponsored post'. The quality of the content affects engagement (likes, shares, comments) – hence it's called 'earned media'.

Customer Lifecycle Journey Continues After-Purchase
It is worth remembering that the previous 'Wow' tactics worked after the customer has experienced the product several times. The journey continues long after the first the initial sale is made.

So stop focusing on separate campaigns, and start thinking about introducing an 'always-on' approach to your marketing. Why? Because your CUSTOMERS DO NOT NECESSARILY MAKE JOURNEYS WHEN YOU DECIDE TO RUN A CAMPAIGN. Customers also use several channels (channels/tactical tools).

Different teams run different channels hence, teams need to collaborate, share the same ultimate goals and help each other so that personalised and relevant messaging can be delivered at each stage of every buyer's journey.

'Always On' requires a real marketing orientation, that instead of over-focusing on YOUR CAMPAIGNS, keeps you close to YOUR CUSTOMER as they move through their lifetime journey.

Owned, Earned and Paid Media - Tactical Choices

Owned Media includes your own website and your own social media platforms. Earned Media is the interactions, the engagement or conversations you earn on your platforms (or elsewhere) from good quality content, while Paid Media is what it says on the tin – advertising which includes both PPC ads and banner ads. Paid Placements (paying to promote your posts and tweets) has now also become part of effective social media tactics.

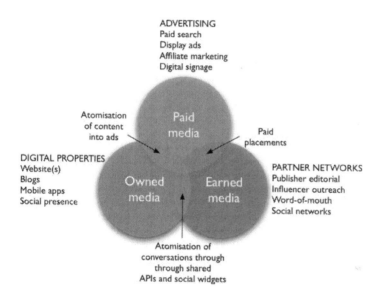

Chaffey and Chadwick (2013)
Owned, Earned and Paid Media – the free ride is over for 'Owned'

Owned, Earned and Paid Media can be integrated, particularly as social media platforms like Facebook are reducing organic reach and forcing marketers to pay for posts to reach wider audiences (paid placements). As Marko Muellner (2013) said 'To influence significant numbers of people via social streams, you need to aggregate large fan communities and then, in many cases, pay per post or share, to increase your campaign scope to existing fans, friends of fans, and beyond. Successful social media advertising requires integrated strategies that consider how organic, earned, and paid media work with content and interactivity to drive outcomes.

They are all inexorably intertwined and must be planned and executed accordingly.' For more, see 'The Rise and Fall Of Owned Earned and Paid Media' on prsmith.org/blog.

Atomization means breaking content into micro assets or bite size chunks (some of which is done automatically through APIs, e.g. posting on a blog automatically triggers a Facebook announcement which in turn triggers a tweet. You can see how easily a survey can be repurposed into a book and then broken into a series of posts, tweets, videos, and infographics. See Section 4.9 for Content Marketing.

Owned, Earned and Paid Media can influence a prospect/customer at various stages of their buying journey. Paid Media is effective at generating awareness and perhaps preference or consideration amongst your target audience, while Earned Media is powerful at helping your prospects and customers to build loyalty and eventually become advocates. Owned Media can help to build consideration as well as deliver a positive customer experience.

For more on Owned, Earned and Paid see, The Rise and Fall Of Owned and Earned But Not Paid Media – World Cup Marketing Wars (prsmith.org/blog). Or if you want to see five different viewpoints try this, 'The difference between paid, owned and earned media – 5 viewpoints' on SmartInsights.com.

The Free Ride Is Over (for 'Owned' Media)

Social Media Marketing was once upon a time 'free'. If you had great content, carefully seeded into the right influencers, at the right time and then released, it could communicate with vast audiences (far bigger than many web sites). Today you have to play to play (to reach your full audience). Perhaps Facebook should now be considered a 'paid channel'.

Which channel?

Go where the conversations are. Identify where your target audience is hanging out. If most of your customers' discussions are on LinkedIn and not Twitter, you should invest more resources on LinkedIn, or if they are using instant chat platforms like WattsApp and WeChat.

Should you invest more in Facebook or not?
What 'great' questions would you ask if you were the marketing manager of a ski holiday company, -Crystal Ski - and you were trying to decide whether it was worth investing more in Facebook or not? What specific questions would you want answering? Remember 'Who, Why and How' might help you. Look away for a few moments and think about what questions you would ask. You can see the full case in an excellent post in Smart Insights.

For now, here are the initial 5 questions:

1. Are you a customer and, if yes, how much do you buy each year?
2. Why do you like our Facebook page (competition/prizes; offers; tips and insights; contact us)

3. After seeing our brand's content in your news feed did you ever feel better about our brand; visit our website; consider buying; buy; tell a friend?
4. How likely would you be to recommend our brand or share the Facebook page?
5. How likely would you be to recommend us to friends and family?

Read this full intriguing example of how ski holiday company, Crystal Ski, asked (and got answers to) some great questions which determined if their Facebook page was worthwhile. See 'Searching For The Real Value Of Facebook Marketing' on the Smart Insights website.

Why are your average sales via Facebook lower than via the website?
In the Crystal Ski case, the average revenue dropped by 18% if the path to conversion included Facebook.

Lots of reasons could explain this, the obvious one being that the occasional flash sales the brand runs reduce the average price of a holiday bought by customers using this channel. So you can learn a lot about your community by asking just a few good questions.

4.5 Which Tactics -The Tactical Matrix

This is another way of deciding which tactical tools to use. Assuming you are clear about what objectives you are trying to achieve, I'm going to show you my Tactical Matrix which is designed to trigger some discussion about which tactical tool is best for you. Firstly, we look at how good each tactic is at moving your prospects/customers through various stages of the Lifetime Buying Process (note this is another variation on some of the other buying models, or stages of buying):

- Awareness
- Consideration
- Purchase
- Post-Purchase Relationship Building
- Post-Purchase Repeat Sales

The need for segmenting your customers or prospects by stage of the buying process emerges again. Now, depending on what stage of the buying cycle you are trying to move your prospects/customers through, you can consider how good each tactic is across these 9 criteria:

- Reach (how big an audience can it reach?)
- Speed (how quickly can it reach that audience?)
- Time (how long to create and deliver this tactic?)
- Message Volume (space to fit message in?)
- Targeting (how granular can the targeting be?)
- Personalization (can the tools personalize?)
- Cost – is it expensive on a Cost Per Thousand (CPT/CPM) basis?
- Control – can you control the message?
- Credibility – some tactics have more credibility.

Tactics Matrix	BENEFIT → TACTIC/ CHANNEL ↓	Reach	Speed	Lead Time	Message Size	Targeting	Personal- ization	Cost CPC/CPM	Control	Credibility (message)
OBJECTIVE ↓										
Awareness/ Familiarity	Display Ads	High	Medium	Long / Med	Medium	High	Medium	Medium	Medium	Low
	PR	High	Medium	Medium	Large	Low	Low	Low	Low	High
	Sponsorship	High	Low / Med	Long	Small	Low	Low	Medium	Low	Medium
	Social media (content marketing)	Low/Med/ High	Low / Med	Medium	Large	Medium	Med / Low	None	Low / Med	High
Consideration	Search Ads & SEO	Low/Med	Medium	Long/Med	Small	High	Medium	Medium	High	Low / Med
	eMail (AM)	Med	High	Short	Large	High	High	Low	High	Medium
	Web Site Incentives	Low/Med	Low	Medium	Med / Low	Low/Med	High with Auto Marketing	None	High	Medium
	Social Media	Low/Med /High	Low	Short / Med	Large	Medium	Med / Low	None	Low / Med	High
	Sales Pitch	Low	Medium	Short	NA	High	High	High	High	Med / High
Decision	Search Ads & SEO	Med / Low	Medium	Short	Small	High	Medium	Medium	High	Low / Med
	eMail (AM)	Medium	High	Short	Large	High	High	Low	High	Medium
	Web Site Incentives	Low	Low	Medium	Low	N/A	High with Auto Marketing	N/A	High	N/A
	Telesales	Low/Med	High	Short / Med	Large	High	High	Low	High	Medium
	Sales Pitch	Low	Medium	Short	Low	High	High	High	High	Med / High
	Exhibition	Medium	Medium	Med/Long	Large	High	Low	High	Medium	Med / High
Post Purchase Relationship Building	Direct Mail/email newsletter/ special offers added value	Medium	High	Short (eM) Med (Dmail)	Large	High	High	Low (eMail) High (DM)	High	Medium
	Social Media	Low/High	Low	Short/Med	Large	High	Medium	None	Low / Med	High
Post Purchase Repeat Sales Loyalty ..Adv..	Direct Mail/eMail	Medium	High	Med/Short	Large	High	High	High (DM)	High	Medium
	Social Media	Low/High	Med	Short/Med	High	High	Medium	None	Low / Med	High

The Tactics Matrix www.PRSmith.org © PR Smith 2014

The Tactics Matrix: you can download this graphic and enlarge it or share it with colleagues from the Tactics Matrix excerpt on my prsmith.org/blog

The last 3 criteria (cost, control [of message] and credibility [of message]) are sometimes used initially when choosing which tactical tool to employ. We know that some tools give you more control over your message (advertising as opposed to PR or even social media), while some tools cost a lot more (direct mail vs advertising) in cost per thousand reached (NB they compare a bit better when looking at cost per eventual conversion). And some tools have more Credibility, e.g. PR, or editorial, has arguably three times more credibility than advertising in the UK while thousands of reviews on social media have, for many, the most credibility.

So, this Tactical Matrix tries to encapsulate all of this – the 10 comms tools, the 5 stages of the buying process and the 9 criteria to help you to choose which tactical tool is best for your plan.

I apologize that this is probably difficult to read here in this book but you can download it from my PRSmith Marketing Blog. It is something of a work in progress, designed to help marketers discuss different criteria when choosing between different tactical tools (or channels). I welcome all comments.

.

4.6 Which Tactics and When

Clearly defined objectives will also help you to decide how to spend your marketing budget (as mentioned, ads, PR and Sponsorship are good at raising awareness, while Selling, Direct Mail and Events were better tactical tools for closing sales).

There are of course exceptions to all of these as social media conversations and reviews (earned media) can create some awareness and certainly help convert visitors to sales and even onto becoming advocates. Here's a Tactics Gantt chart summarizing what happens when (and how much is spent).

The Gantt Chart on the next page shows a bird's eye view of which tactical tools happen when and for how much

So, you have to decide which tactical tools (or channels) to allocate your resources to (and when), and within each tactical tool you have to choose which vehicle or, in the case of social media, which particular social media platform?

Which Tactical Tools When (& how much budget)

	J	F	M	A	M	J	J	A	S	O	N	D	€/$
Website	x	x											25k
Develop			x	x	x	x			x	x	x	x	5k
Forums			xx	xx	xx	xx	x	xx	xx	xx	xx	xx	30k
Social Media	x	x	xx	xx	xx	xx	x	xx	xx	xx	xx	xx	15k
SEO	x	x								xx			
Advertising:													
Display Ads		x	x	xx		xx	xx	xx	x	xx	xx	xx	xx xx	25k
Pay Per Click	x	x	xx	xx	xx	xx	x	xx	xx	xx	xx	xx	30k
Ads	x	x		xx	xx	xx		xx	x	xx	xx	xx	xx xx	30k
Facebook Ads	x	x		x	x			x		x	x	x	x	
		x						x					
Online sponsorship	x	x	x	x	x	x	x	x	x	x	x	x	10k
Public Relations			x		x		x	x	x		x		10k
News Releases						x	x						
Viral Marketing													
Direct Mail													
Opt-In email		x		xx		xx				xx		xx	20k
(NB retention		x											
v acquisition)													
Sales Promotion/			x			x			x			x	10k
Competition													
Online Events			x	x						x	x		50k
Virtual										x			20k
Exhibitions													20k
Affiliate													
Events													
Total													300k

Marketing Communications Gantt Chart

The good news is that your analytics makes these decisions a lot easier as it enables you to make more informed decisions about which tactical tools (channels) are delivering you the best results.

Your analytics tells you where your traffic is coming from, which tactical channel (ads, SEO, email, links, social media etc.) even which social media channel. So, if you get more visitor traffic from, say, Facebook on a particular topic or type of content it may be worthwhile spending some budget promoting these type of posts to get even more traction-particularly if the visitors from these sources actually convert to registrations, enquiries or sales. More on Analytics (and multichannel funnel analytics) in the 'Control' section.

4.7 Tactical Targeting - More Bangs For Your Buck

Customer profiling helps tactical targeting

The success of your tactics is partly dependent upon how good your targeting skills are.

It is worth spending time considering carefully what is your ideal customer profile(s) and how you might find more of them using a variety of new tools available.

Detailed customer profiling makes it easier to find more customers when you:

Target direct mail and email via databases with similar types of customers.

Target ads at very specific customer profiles.

Target social selling at very specific customer profiles.

Target similar customer profiles

You can find similar 'ideal customer profiles' by inserting (or 'indexing') the attributes of your best customers (or even just the attributes of the best converters on your site) to find additional ideal prospects from external third-party databases like Net Mining' and Adjug Ad Exchange. They profile your customers and then give you similar ones from their own databases.

Target ads at very specific customer profiles

You can now target very specific audiences. For example, on Facebook or Linkedin, you can find prospects with similar preferences as your own customers ('lookalikes').

You can also 'custom' using up to 200 variables to build your very specific target audiences   e.g. target by location (country, state, city, postcode); networks (people whose friends are connected to your page, people already connected); interests (business, hobbies, fitness/wellness, entertainment) and right down to games, movies or the music they like; behaviour (travel, mobile device, digital activities); demographics (age, gender, language and education, generation, work, relationship status) and a lot more.

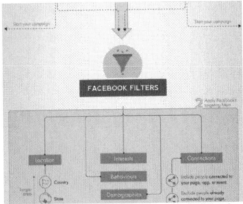

Courtesy of Qwaya – See full infographic & discussion
on prsmith.org/blog How To Target Very Specific Audiences

Both Facebook and LinkedIn allow you to target ads and/or promoted posts by interests, age, geographic locations and a lot more (as shown in the many Facebook 'filters').

Or you can target specific types of visitors to your website (customers that visit certain pages can be retargeted with specific and relevant ads after they have left your site as they move around other sites that are within the same advertising network (e.g. Google Ads network).

Warning

Some major brands think Micro Targeting loses the broader awareness, intrigue and prestige which a brand can build with a wider audience.

Social Selling: Target prospects talking about a particular topic via social media and third-party databases

. People who hashtag a particular word or acronym (adding # before a word or acronym) flag the word up as important in their discussion so that anyone else can easily join the conversation 'thread' about the hashtagged word.

Drawing on major third-party database owners and searching across social media platforms, these people can be quickly identified and filtered by country, language, company type, company size and even an individual's interest.

Target prospects talking about your key topics

Social Monitoring Streams can be set up for each sales rep with a list of their leads.

They are immediately notified when any of these leads mention your company name, or any of the topics mentioned above.

Who are the frequent flyers who might take a train instead?

If you were trying to sell train tickets to frequent flyers - who are the ideal prospects? Your ability to ask great questions, find databases and interrogate them in new ways to profile prospects is a great skill. Look away. Stop and think for a moment.

How about asking data owners of major mobile networks (e.g. WEVE) to find 'mobile users who disappear in Heathrow and reappear in Edinburgh in the time a flight would take'. Then segment these travellers and promote highly relevant offers via their mobiles. Add a mobile commerce component enabling prospects to directly purchase a rail ticket, or just wave their smartphone at the ticket counter or transport kiosk. (SAS, 2014) Could mobile technologies be the future of retail? Source: PR Smith 2015 NB Although WEVE have since stopped offering this service, it does demonstrate a different type of data usage to profile prospects. As always, check anything you do is GDPR compliant.

Target conference event attendees talking about #topic
You can find prospects in a particular conversation, e.g. delegates' tweets at conferences or events usually include the conference or event hashtag. Instead of buying that expensive attendees list from the event organizer, run a 60 second search for a conference hashtag via an agency (or

consultancy) and get email, phone and social data – which can be further filtered by geographic region, e.g. a search for anyone tweeting about #InfoSec (the Information Security Technical Conference) delivers a delegate list of 1,104 delegates' email addresses, job titles, locations, company sizes (via a 'matching engine' that cross references and checks against other databases and social platforms with 95% accuracy). An automated marketing campaign can then target tailored relevant information to this hot target list.

 # Hashtags How interest in one topic may translate into interest in another

People group topics together so it's useful to see what topics/key phrases relate to each other. Hashtagify.me website shows you what hashtags are being used in conjunction with one another. How interest in one topic may translate to another. (Murphy, 2013). This site (followerwonk) identifies influencers for any hashtag and also searches for common interests with these influencers making it easier to connect with them.

Target specific prospects via instigating conversation - social selling

After clearly defining the 'ideal customer' profile, set up a new LinkedIn page, register as a LinkedIn Pro and using Boolean coding to carefully target and invite, say, 300 prospects pcm. to join highly relevant discussions (for their specific industry sector).

Say, on average 100+ join. Phase 2 roll starts some good conversations. Phase 3 invites members for a 1-2-1 Skype chat re: specific solutions that the prospect is interested in. This can generate up to ten highly qualified leads pcm.

Some marketers believe social media is about helping and not about selling; I feel it is down to how relevant and useful the discussions are. It all comes back to helping the customer. NB This approach to social selling probably doesn't work so well today as it did just a few years ago.

Target specific prospects by social interests, technologies or skills

Prospects can also be targeted via their enterprise systems, e.g. show me contacts from all companies who are using a particular technology (e.g. 'Salesforce'), who are located in London, where contacts have a job function of marketing or sales at a senior level (director) and are interested in sales and marketing alignment.

This might only produce a small list of prospects but it can be a valuable list of hot prospects. Once you find them, then engage with these contacts on a highly personalized level, either via email, direct mail, telephone or on social media.

Target specific prospects by engaging in existing #topic conversations and using personalised videos

By listening carefully for any conversations across all main social media channels e.g. using a   hashtag Red Dwarf, Tim Redgate (Time Redgate Consultancy) was able to identify individuals discussing the TV Series, Red Dwarf, and within minutes join the conversation by sending a personalised video to each individual. They could target individuals with a minimum of 500 followers and they could do this at scale (more than 50,000 personalised videos per hour). The recipient of the video can choose to delete or, as in the majority of cases the recipient proudly shares his/her personalised trailer.

Personalsied videos at scale: the trailer video for Red Dwarf tailored for Mark Luke Dixon was done at scale.

Target better quality visitors with SEO

Sometimes conversion rates are low because you may be attracting the wrong type of visitor. Perhaps less volume of visitors but better quality of visitors can improve your situation. I mentioned the importance of Search Engine Optimization in chapter 1 and it is worth remembering that although high quality SEO will get you more visitors by being listed high up in search engine results pages (SERPS) for phrases that your ideal customers are using, it does require resources (skills, budgets and time) .

The SEO budget may be spread across to social media as occasionally, some staff have a joint responsibility for SEO and social media marketing since SEO today is more dependent on good quality content and social media marketing than the technical aspects of SEO.

Target influencers

If you are opening a sushi restaurant in New York – you can find the most influential sushi Twitter users within a radius of 10 miles and then start interacting with them. Analyze your members' interests – then personalize your messages.

See what the best time to tweet is. What topics are most popular with them? Then target this list with a DM campaign (direct message via Twitter). You can also do this with your competitor's community – tracking their followers every day. Or do this with the whole Twitter community or with those that tweet with a particular hashtag or even just a word, or a link.

Tweetreach measures the total number of impressions generated by tweets, who saw them and who helped to spread the word. Tweetreach uses advertising language such as 'reach' and 'impressions'.

Other tools like SocialBro cover some of the 'Who, Why and How' questions including: Who has followed and unfollowed you? Who are your influencers - listed according to level of influence, location, gender, how active they are on Twitter? I've mentioned followerwonk.com which also identifies influencers that are following you, or you can just create a list of influencers in your Twitter account.
One of many social media dashboards, Hootsuite, helps you to monitor and converse with multiple social platforms including Facebook, LinkedIn, Twitter and more via a single dashboard.
*Blogger Outreach Programmes identify and work with Opinion Formers. See digital guru Zaid Al Zaidy, talking about how agencies use 'Blogger Outreach' programmes.

Here's a few useful influencer marketing tools:

- Gorkana.com lists UK journalist & influencers and their credentials

- Little Bird GetlittleBird.com identifies relevant influencers in a location on a topic (USA).

- Webfluential.com/marketers finds influencers across the world.

Zaid Al Zaidy talking about <u>Blogger Outreach Programmes</u> on YouTube PRSmith1000 channel

4.8 The Magic Marketing Formula

Whichever tactical tools (or channels) you use and whether manual or automated communications, always apply my Magic Marketing Formula - IRD - to boost results.

- **Identify** needs.
- **Reflect** these needs and benefits (through ads, sales presentations, search engines etc.)
- **Deliver** a good customer experience (i.e. fulfill your promise consistently at every touch point).

If Coca-Cola identify that people need to be loved, they reflect this by showing ads of people drinking Coke and having a good time (whether polar bears or people) and all feeling happy and being loved.

If a B2B IT supplier identifies a segment's main need is, say, security, then it reflects 'security' in its ads, exhibitions, social media and optimizes for these key phrases.

A simpler example is obvious with the search engines and the magic marketing formula when you search for a very specific multi-word key phrase and then you see the exact phrase appear in the Search Engine results. It is a eureka moment. It's like a fusion of your specific need with a supplier's offering. The perfect match.

This is the formula reflecting your needs (phrases) through SEO.

A shocking example of the Magic Marketing Formula
Here's a shocking example of the Magic Marketing Formula in action. Road deaths from speeding drivers is an issue in Northern Ireland. In-depth research by the Department of the Environment, revealed that speeders feel it is their right to drive at whatever speed they want.

They won't change this for anything. 'What about if you killed someone?' No this wouldn't stop them. 'What if you killed a child?' A resounding chilling silence. The idea was born. The ad reflected the horror of killing a child.

A shockvertisement that stops drivers from speeding
See this shock video prsmith.org

The ad went viral. Millions are watching it. Speeders are slowing down. With the economic cost of a death estimated at £1.68m and the campaign cost of £400,000 you can see that this ad can be justified on a purely economic basis.

On an emotional basis you might find this disturbing, but it does increase awareness and, most importantly, change behaviour. In fact, AdWeek praised the 60 second ad for "driving the anti-speeding message into the public conversation far beyond Ireland."

You can see this stats and more on this campaign including how it went viral and the research that went into it on 'Research Driven Shock Ad Uses Magic Formula and Goes Viral' at prsmith.org/blog.

The challenge – moving from campaigns to customer life cycles
The challenge, it seems, is to, somehow, move away from campaigns to conversations. In fact, continuing conversations across owned, earned and paid media. This is particularly true if the buying cycle lasts longer than the campaign period. Marketing Automation can help here.

Constant conversations, content marketing and marketing automation ('Always On')

In the quest for constant relevant conversation with both existing customers and new prospects, 24/7, 365 days of the year, marketing automation has a role to play, particularly if there is a stream of relevant and interesting content being produced. We will look at the actual process required to develop great content and develop your marketing automation in the Actions chapter.

Email behavioural responses such as 'opens' (of the email) and 'click-throughs' (to the links in the email) are also recorded so that those that don't open the email automatically get a second email with a different message in the subject line and those that did open the email but didn't click through automatically get a completely different second email message.

Effectively, every visit and every interaction online can be added over time to learn more about the customer, progressively improve the visitor's profile and automatically deliver more relevant content.

Marketing automation requires a set of rules (e.g. if a visitor clicks this and then watched the full video – they then get served this particular piece of content. .

Continuously striving to improve this process, embraces the Magic Marketing Formula. For example, a mail shot invites prospects to download a report. Those that respond submit their industry sector in the form. The next email then offers some extremely relevant content such as a free report about that specific industry sector.

You want content to continually add value to your customer journeys.

How do you decide which content to create and how to get it into the hands of your target audience?

Read on.

4.9 Content Marketing

Content Marketing is a major component of your customers' experience as you help them along their journey. Content can be a source of differentiation, or even a source of competitive advantage. It can attract visitors, help to nurture them into customers and help to retain them.

Content Marketing is all about creating and distributing, at the right time, really relevant content (videos, infographics, power point slides, tweets, posts, articles, white papers, books and even games) that helps prospects and customers to achieve their goals (e.g. skills improvement or being informed or entertained).

Your choice of content ('content strategy') is influenced by your mission, your brand values and brand personality and also what your customers want or would value, that your competitors don't currently share.

Think like a publisher

You have to think like a publisher, discover hot topics that are not well served by competitors, brain storm, create content concepts, select the best ones, produce them, distribute them and measure their impact. See the range of content in the content pyramid in 'How Integrated Content Marketing Creates Competitive Advantage (Smith 2014).

You need a team that looks like an egg timer (large at the start, thin in the middle and large at the end. A cross-functional group at the beginning (for brain storming), then a small editorial team and small production team to produce the content, and finally a large team mobilized to help the distribution (and engagement) at the end. Sometimes called **'Content Distribution'**.

Why not ask your partners, resellers and suppliers to **spread your content**? GaggleAmp alerts these groups every time you post, makes it easy for them to share and rewards them for sharing. It also integrates with marketing automation systems. Costs $100 pcm if you regularly post content (or less if you are infrequent).

Leverage your content
Your marketing and advertising team probably have a lot of material that they can share on Instagram. Sharing advertising collateral and any marketing content (PR photos with an added caption) in an organic way simply gets you 'more bangs for your buck'.

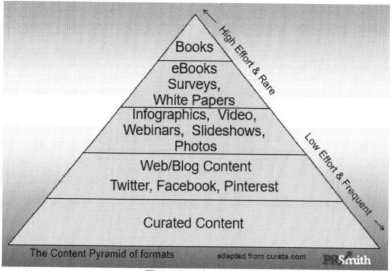

The content pyramid

Surprisingly, a well-produced printed book (with excellent graphics and production value, and assuming good content) is top of the content pyramid (if its relevant).

A blog post's key points can be broken into many tweets etc. Images can be re-used in many ways. You leverage, across many tactical channels, the assets you invested in and created (rather than leave them gathering dust). See Kelly's HR example. NB Some content is better for certain tasks. See Dave Chaffey's Smart Insights Content Matrix (on the next page).

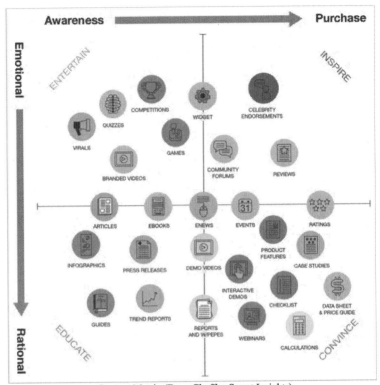

Content Matrix (Dave Chaffey Smart Insights)

Sift through your assets and then polish and release them in an organized process (or schedule). See Kelly HR for a full case study of how a team of two generated content from one piece of research to fuel content for books, blog posts, tweets, infographics, videos, public talks and a lot more (see content pyramid) – all went global and connected with a very specific universe of HR Directors globally.

See Kelly HR for a full case study prsmith.org/blog

Evergreen Content & Optimising Historical Content

Improving, updating and optimising old posts with evolving concepts and contemporary key phrases helps to keep them current. Identifying

---

Great Views Lousy Conversion (poor photo replaced)!

A beauty treatment product was getting great views, but lousy conversion, the reason was simply found to be a poor product shot which was easily remedied. Chaffey (2018)

Content Wars

Customers are drowning in a sea of content. Competitors are churning out content – some good and some bad. Customers' ability to consume content is finite because there are only so many hours in a day to read/watch/listen, even to really interesting content.

Content Wars rage while customers drown in a sea of content

Content Saturation and 'Content Shock'

Mark Schaefer (2014) describes this as the 'Content Shock' when 'At some point, the amount I am "paying out" will exceed the amount I am bringing in and at that point, creating content will not be a smart business decision for me and many other businesses.'

Content Shock has a common pattern: as the volume of posts/articles grows in this case, on the topic of 'Content Marketing', the average number of shares declines well before 'Content Saturation' i.e. when the number of articles peaks.

We may have to pay customers to read our content! In fact, we already do (indirectly as we spend, say 6 hours writing a blog post at a nominal cost of £100 per hour = £600 spent producing the piece!).'

Content marketing should be designed so that it is **easy to measure its impact** (is it driving traffic, or is it boosting registrations or sales?).

It also must have feedback mechanisms beyond KPIs and analytics, which allow customers to give direct feedback.

Build **'Content Pathways'** so that when prospects or customers show interest in (open) a particular piece of content, they automatically get sent another, even more relevant, piece of content (or a link to a piece of content).

Content marketing can be a major component in your strategy. But in a hyper-competitive environment you need to have processes in place to monitor **which kind of content works best**. See the interview regarding 'content marketing and analytics' in the Control section for more. Plus what is the best way of distributing your best content. Content Distribution can be as important as the content itself!

Great quality content can deliver low-cost visitors and conversions but it may be worth pushing your best content via paid media (e.g. sponsored posts and ads) as they can generate additional conversions. It is worth testing and subsequently blending. In fact, you need to test and blend both.

So there are many existing and new tactical tools to help marketers. Now let us explore the execution of the tactics in the chapter called 'Actions'.

And before we go to 'Actions' section, ask one more question......

Are you more interesting than my wife?

Many people allow personal emails and business emails into their in box. So, your commercial email message is not competing with other suppliers, you are also competing with everyone for my attention - from my wife or my best friend to my business colleagues and other competing suppliers. As I scan my emails, I see one from my wife and amidst the other emails, I see your email. The crunch question first coined by Jay Bear (2013) is: 'Is your company (email) more interesting to me than my wife?' Does your subject/title or headline really cut through the clutter?

Chapter 5 Actions

Strategy summarizes, and gives direction to, 'How you are going to get there?' Tactics are the details of strategy and Actions are the details of tactics. The Actions section of your plan ensures that the tactics are executed with excellence and passion.

The Actions section of your plan is often forgotten. Hence, we get a lot of sloppy execution: sloppy web sites, emails, experiences. Actions is all about ensuring your staff and external agencies will execute your plan with passion and excellence. How?

Internal Marketing
Internal marketing is critical to ensure excellent execution. It involves:
- Communication
- Motivation
- Training

Internal Marketing is all about taking time to bring your team with you. Understanding their worries (AI will take my job); Understanding what motivates your staff (how you can win their buy-into your plan), then communicating clearly and frequently (whether by face-to-face or internal communications systems), and finally, training staff to ensure everyone has the skills to execute the new plan. Essentially explain and motivate the team so that everyone knows who has to do what, when and how.

Staff need training to know how to use:
- Systems & Processes
- Guidelines & Checklists
- Mini Action Plans (project plans)
- Constant Optimisation

This can include mini action plans since each tactic is a mini project which needs professional execution. You don't have to include all the mini projects in your marketing plan.

You can add systems, processes, guidelines and checklists, either into the body of the plan or in the appendices at the back, or you can simply issue them later. But, it is worth listing in the Actions section which guides and checklists need to be produced. This section of your plan is about ensuring that your plan is executed to a high standard.

Here's The Bad News
'Everything degenerates into work.'
Peter Drucker

Why deliver sloppy customer experiences?
How many brands do not execute their plans to a high standard? How much money is wasted driving traffic to a website that frustrates visitors? How many service chatbots leave you wanting to pull your hair out? 'Develop credibility before raising visibility', i.e. do your website usability testing before promoting the site. Lousy execution not only wastes scarce resources but also destroys the customer experience and, hence, destroys the brand. The ad spend is, effectively, destroying the brand! Mobilise your team. Inject purpose and passion for excellence.

'Firms Of Endearment' Outperform Other Businesses
World-Class companies profit from passion and purpose. They endear themselves to customers and communities. All staff are made fully aware of the overall mission and

purpose of the business. Over 10 years S&P 500 grew by 122% while Firms of Endearment grew by over 1000%.

Excellent Execution = Competitive Advantage

If your team really want to execute strategy and tactics better than your competitors you can create competitive advantage -just through better Action/Execution. A former CEO of GE and a Harvard Business Professor actually wrote a book claiming that an organization's ability to execute (better than their competitors) generates competitive advantage. They called it "Execution: The discipline of getting things done", by Larry Bossidy and Ram Charan (2012).

> **'Vision without execution is just hallucination.'**
> Henry Ford

To help to execute each tactic it helps if the tactic has its own detailed objectives, an allocated budget, a list of who does what, when and, ideally, an estimate of the return generated by the tactic – whether this is sales generated, number of visitors, level of engagement (number of Likes, shares, comments) or even level of awareness generated, or level of preference generated.

You can put a financial value on each of these including awareness levels (greater awareness = greater market share), the value of a Like, even just a visit or moving prospects through the funnel (e.g. from home page to product demonstration).

This is good practice and you can see how tactics, action and control start to overlap. SOSTAC® is just an easy-to-remember, logical structure for the sections of your plan. Adjust it as you see fit.

I'll spend a little more time on the processes involved in both Content Marketing and also Marketing Automation as they are two 'hot' topics right now.

So I will briefly show you the 'actions' required to make these happen. The rest, we'll cover with just a few paragraphs.

Internal marketing
Spending time and money communicating your plans to your internal teams, motivating them to get behind your plans and ensuring they know how to execute the plan (training). Some companies spend 10% -15% of their marketing budget ensuring their staff understand, believe in and become capable of executing the plan.

Many companies are dysfunctional and siloed to a greater or lesser degree. Plus, most staff have a **neurotic resistance to change** and any new ideas.

Incidentally, this is partly why 50% of the world's largest CRM (Customer Relationship Management) projects fail (people resist change).

Communicating, motivating and training your staff is the key to great execution. Are all of your staff fully behind your social media efforts and your AI Chatbots development? Will they seed your marketing content where appropriate (will they send some of your content to the influencers in their own networks)?

Do your staff really believe in your product or service?
Do you make them feel proud of it?
Do they feel proud of it?

Internal Marketing Acid Test
If B2C, how many of your staff are brand advocates?

5.1 Communication

You need to allocate time and budget to communicating with your team whether it is 1-2-1 meetings, town square meetings, webcasts, emails, letters, phone calls… you need to ensure that everyone who needs to know about your plan, knows about it.

5.2 Motivation

You need to know how to motivate your team, particularly when it comes to new processes or new systems. Staff often resist new tasks. Partly because of lack of motivation and partly because they don't know how to use them (training).

Here is an example of a highly motivated brand advocate staff member who made a shockvertisement for his company.

This man is sufficiently motivated that he made his own 'Shockvertising' video for his company, Bissell Canada? prsmith.org/blog

He uses his Bissell floor cleaner to clean a space on the platform floor in the subway (underground train), then pours his curry dinner onto the floor and then eats his dinner! Will this start a surge of employee product demo ads?

Do not try this at home! Beware, you may find this video revolting (you can see it on prsmith.org/blog).

5.3 Training

Also remember, even if staff are motivated, they have to have the right skills across a range of new marketing roles in an ever-changing marketing team.

Do staff have the skills to use the new CRM system, to integrate with chatbots, to upload content into the marketing automated system? Can they manage a mini project? Staff need training, so they can use:

- Systems & Processes (e.g. marketing automation)
- Guidelines & Checklists (e.g. social media usage)
- Mini Action Plans (e.g. roject plans)
- Constant Optimisation (e.g. beta testing)

5.3.1 Systems & Processes

Let's look at what is the process or system required to
to set up and run Marketing Automation.

Introducing a Marketing Automation System

Once upon a time a sales person could watch a buyer's
body language to see what really interested the buyer and
whether they were ready to buy. Today sales people rarely
see buyers face-to-face as buyers do a lot of their buying
online. Marketers can, however, see each potential buyer's
digital body language which identifies at what stage in the
buying process the visitor is and whether they are ready to
buy. Your click behaviour leaves a trail of your interests,
what engaged you, what didn't, and more.

Digital body language

Marketing automation analyses each visitor's digital body
language (their click behaviour) and gives each visitor a
particular score which is determined by how interested they
are in which products/services.

For example, someone who bounces off the first page
(exits) might get a minus score; someone who stays 5
minutes looking at product pages gets a higher score, and
someone else who looks at product pages, leaves the site
and later comes back and watches the product video and
moves to the shopping basket (but doesn't buy) gets an
even higher score.

These scores and rules allow the system to automatically
respond with tailored relevant messages offering more
information or help required via the visitor's preferred
channel whether a dynamic web page, a pop-up message,
an email, a text or even a request to a rep to phone the
prospect.

Marketing automation systems help organizations automatically engage with their prospects and customers at the right time, with the right content, via the right channel.

A simple sample marketing automation system

A screen grab of an intriguing video clip with attention grabbing headline is posted across several platforms as part of the continuous inbound marketing campaign. This generates inbound traffic with just one click. Those that watch the video are asked, at the end, if they'd like alerts re similar videos and reports. A percentage of visitors do so.

Step 1: Visitor registers name, email and industry sector.
Step 2: Email them an invitation to download a free report.
Step 3: Send a thank you to the people who visited the site and downloaded the report.
Step 4: Send them a case study from their industry.
Step 5: Prospects that click on the case study, get a 'lead score' or 'grade' (depending on their click behavior/digital body language and/or other information collected).
Step 6: Sales rep gets an auto alert regarding high grade prospects that deserve a follow up.

See Account Based Marketing (mentioned in the Strategy section under 'Target Markets').

The steps required to set up a Marketing Automation programme:

1. Clearly define the stages of a sale (and after sale) e.g. visitor/prospect - lead - enquiry - customer - advocate.
2. Define and score digital behaviour required for each stage of a sale e.g. opening a particular email; visiting a particular page(s); downloading a white

paper.
3. Clarify what behaviour/score triggers what response.
4. Agree next auto steps for customers that respond ('responders' and 'non-responders').

Once this detailed process is rigorously completed an MA programme can:

- integrate social media, direct mail/email, telemarketing and more
- continually serve tailored and highly relevant web landing pages to different visitors
- continually respond via dynamic web pages, dynamic emails, pop up messages
- alert sales or customer service people to call customers

All this without needing assistance from the IT team. You can also set up A/B tests as part of this process to see which pages/offers/photos convert better. The original book on digital body language was written by Steven Woods (co-founder of Eloqua) back in 2009.

Systems & Processes

RFM Database Analysis

Which customers on your database are more likely to keep buying from you? Which customers are worth spending more time and money on (more communications and more rewards)? As mentioned in the Situation Analysis section, database marketers have, for many decades now, used RFM (Recency, Frequency, Monetary) to identify those active customers that are more likely to continue buying throughout their customer lifetime. The ones you might want to invest in - these 'ideal customers'.

Recent customers are more likely to have more active relationships than those who haven't purchased for several years. Equally, more frequent purchasers are more likely to continue purchasing. Monetary means size of purchase - on average, bigger spenders are more likely to buy again than small spenders. Latency is often added. Latency means the average duration between purchases. Customers with shorter latency are more likely to purchase again. Many organizations combine RFM to score customers in order to identify which segments of customers are more likely to respond positively.

Here's how it can be used: take 'Recency'. Calculate the average 'recency of purchase' for your customers. Then create two groups: (1) 'More Recent Than Average' - those customers with average frequency and also those with 'more recent' than average frequency. (2) 'Less Recent Than Average' - those customers whose last visit or purchase is less recent than average. Group 2 ('Less Recent') is most likely to be in the process of defecting (or have already defected). Group 1 ('More Recent') can have a 3-10 times higher response rate. So invest in these.

	More Recent	Less Recent
Customer Source:		
Search Engines	70% of visitors	30% of visitors
Emails	30% of visitors	70% of visitors

Say, customers generated by search engines and customers generated by email deliver the same current value. Each dollar spent on either channel is equally profitable. It is also worth checking the potential value of each type of customer, e.g. the potential lifetime value of search visitors might be much higher than visitors generated via email.

Current value and potential value
It is possible to segment your customers using many variables, including media used to acquire a customer; keyword phrase used to find the site; content areas visited. It often takes more than one visit to a site before a visitor converts and buys.

The 'How' section explores how we can analyze customer journeys to identify which channels are worth investing more resources in. See Novo, J. - WebTrends Take 10 Series Increase Customer Retention by Analyzing Visitor Segments,

Predicting your customers' future needs
In addition to RFM, purchases can be anticipated by 'time triggers', e.g. six months after a car is bought it needs its first service.

'Date triggered' purchases means a particular date like a birthday or a seasonal event like Father's Day or Christmas Day triggers purchasing of all sorts of products and services.

'Purchase triggered' purchases occur when buying one product suggests the need for a supporting product/service, e.g. when you buy a car you also might want to buy a warranty and certainly, insurance.

Basketball's low hanging fruit

Database Analysis Identifies the Best Targets – the most likely, least likely and fence sitters.

Professional basketball clubs such as <u>Orlando Magic</u> now analyze their season ticket holders by exploring historic purchasing data and renewal patterns to:

'build decision tree models that bucket subscribers into three categories:
- most likely to renew,
- least likely and
- fence sitters.

The fence sitters then get the customer service department's attention come renewal time.'

5.3.2 Issuing Guidelines & Checklists (training)

Social Media Guidelines
These can include attitude, tone, topics, content type, confrontation (how to avoid it) and frequency.

Follow the 4-1-1 Rule from <u>Tipping point Labs and Joe Pulizzi</u> of the Content Marketing Institute which states, 'For every one self-serving tweet, you should retweet one relevant tweet and most importantly, share four pieces of relevant content written by others.'

Guidelines will include etiquette online – what you can and cannot say. No foul language. No abusive comments. No trade secrets nor sensitive information revealed.

In fact, many guides suggest you should stay positive, despite what comments are thrown at you. Some other guides specify that you must not criticize competition directly.
Some guides include key messages, key phrases and/or social media details. Many organizations issue guidelines before a new campaign or initiative starts.

Brand personality and values should be included although a full Brand Guidelines can run into 100 pages, so it is best just to list the key brand guidelines such as personality and values.

Here is <u>The 10-Point Social Media Checklist / Policy Everyone Will Understand</u> written by Jeff Roach (2014) after a client, the tenth person this year, asked him, if he could help them draft a social media policy for their company (see next page).

Social Media - Author Checklist

1	Be kind.	
2	You are a person first, an employee second.	
3	Spend most of your time listening and liking (and helping), not posting.	
4	Expectations for professional conduct are the same online as offline (do not criticize a competitor, use foul language etc.).	
5	Do not embarrass or disparage the company.	
6	Do not share private or confidential information (e.g. trade secrets).	
7	Understand your privacy settings but know that any post can accidentally become public.	
8	Pay attention to and support your colleagues' posts.	
9	Be mindful of the reputation you are creating.	
10	Be yourself.	

Social Media - Management Checklist

1	Clarify the organization's social media objectives.	
2	Clarify the customer experience you want your audiences to enjoy.	
3	Clarify any staff responsibilities whether: (a) optional (e.g. tweet about the company's sales promotions) or	
4	(b) compulsory (e.g. add social media addresses to all email signatures in a consistent style).	
5	Clarify what identify security measures: (a) who has access to which platforms or	
6	(b) how passwords are stored and updated.	
7	Announce where social media integrates with: (a) other company policies (e.g. HR, PR)	
8	(b) other company marketing comms tools (e.g. ad campaigns and news releases). (c) Introduce style guides for consistent TOV (Tone Of Voice) & relevant topics only. See Mailchimp Style Guide.	
9	Build in crisis planning for senior management: explain how social media can help and hinder during a crisis.	
10	Always check your social advice checklists with your legal team.	

LinkedIn Checklist

Checklists help knowledge transfer and ensure skills are shared around an organization. It's also good contingency/continuity planning (what if a key person leaves, or is ill?).

Here's a very simple five point checklist for using LinkedIn from Jason Miller (2013) This can, and should be, developed into a much more detailed checklist. However, it is a good starting point.

1	Optimize Your LinkedIn Page	
2	Engage Your Audience	
3	Attract More Followers	
4	Follow the 4-1-1 Rule (see social media guidelines)	
5	Analyze	

Better Understanding Of Needs = Better Content

Instead of offering British exporters a newsletter packed with general export advice and a range of case studies, UK Trade and Investment now offer businesses interested in China a newsletter about exporting to China, and a separate newsletter about exporting to Russia for businesses interested in Russia. UKTI now get much higher open rates and traders rate it more highly. Less is more.

Visual Opportunity Checklist
exploiting the shift to visual media

1	Don't tell if you can show	
2	Create Original Visual Content	
3	Showcase your story: images = emotion and connection	
4	Crowd Source Visual Content: engage fans to create and share images for you; connect and promote your brand visually; contribute to photo and video competition, events	
5	Add back the words: add captions, descriptions; overlay with call to action; add keywords and hashtags to image descriptions; include watermark or website url on original images	
6	Mix it up: overlay text on instagrams; tweet images and Pinterest pins on Twitter; pin videos to Pinterest; Use more images on Facebook; include quality images on blog posts	

Source: Dalton (2012) How brands can leverage the power of visual social media, Media Matters, 20 Dec.

5.3.3 Mini Action Plans (project plans)

When executing each tactic it helps to keep everyone
focused on doing a good job if the tactic has its own
detailed objectives, a budget, responsibilities and estimated
returns.

Here are two examples of how tactics cascade down into
actions and details. One is from a Facebook ad campaign
and the other from a Twitter ad campaign (both are from
Smart Insights 'Party Central Plan').

Facebook Ad Campaign

Tactic	Objective	Action	Who	When	Budget
Face-book ad cam-paign	Increase traffic from 250,000 unique visitors per month to 400,000 pcm over a 12 month period.	Sign up for Face-book ads, select specific products to use for pro-moted stories and trial for one month	Dig Mktg Mngr	April 2020	£ 50,000

The Facebook page includes a 'new products' section and our Google Analytics shows us that this drives an average of:

1,000 new sales to our website each month (1%).

Whilst this is low, these are higher spending visitors with an average spend of £150.

They particularly buy the 'colour sets' (e.g. coral earrings, matching necklace and bangles) and 30% opt for the express delivery service.

For ads, we're estimating a £1.12 cost per click with a 0.5% clickthrough rate and a lower average basket of £40.

This indicates we exceed our £800k target, but as this is a trial, we will need to adjust after month 1.

Media	Budget £	Estimated cost per click	Click-through rate %	Potential reach	Actual Click-through	Average basket £	Sales generated £
Face-book	2,500 00	1.12	0.5	4,464, 286	22,321	40	892, 857

This will cover the cost of the campaign and generate additional likes, which will in turn, generate further sales.

Twitter Ad Campaign

Tactic	Objective	Action	Who	When	Budget
Twitter ad campaign	Drive 17,000 more visitors to the website to generate £600,000 sales	Sign up for Twitter ads, select specific products to use for promoted tweets and trial for one month	Dig Mktg Mngr	May 2020	£ 15,000

Google Analytics shows us that Twitter drives an average of 10% new visitors to our website each month. So, 35,000 fans deliver 3,500 visitors a month, with a higher conversion rate of 1% (they will be shown an image before clicking) and a higher spend rate (£72 per basket).

Our campaign will focus on promoted tweets, selected by Twitter. A monthly budget of £15,000 is thought to be able to generate £1 million in sales – this would exceed the additional £800k pcm target. It's based on an average basket of £60, but as we haven't done this before, it could be much lower, so our numbers are based on a lower than average basket of £35.

Media	Budget £	Estimated cost per click	Click-through rate %	Potential reach	Click-throughs	Average basket £	Sales Generated £
Twitter	15,000	0.85	3	588,235	17,647	35	617,647

5.3.4 Constant Optimisation

Develop a constant beta culture. Surround yourself with people who become interested in seeing how small changes can make small improvements. 0.5% improvement here and 0.5% improvement there, soon adds up. Constantly split testing ads, emails and landing pages to see if particular phrases, words, images or colours make a difference. This is so important, I'm going to repeat it in the final Control section.

People will become fascinated when they can see, almost immediately, how a change that they make affects the online results.

This constant beta culture becomes infectious and nurtures the inquisitive mind: 'What if we tried this...?' as everything can be easily tested.

Remember results do not lie Watching actual results coming in stops subjective arguments. Everyone sees actual changes in traffic, conversions and repeat sales. Here's how simplifying a form, reduced 'form friction' (anger created by large forms) boosted sales by 2000%.

"Facebook has over 10,000 versions of facebook being tested continuously."

Mark Zuckerberg, facebook founder in a Masters of Scale interview with Read Hoffman

---

Simplifying sign-up forms

HSBC's old registration page had become a barrier –
asking too many questions (too early in the relationship).

The form below, with its 17 fields of data, generated just
two enquiries per week. The long list of questions irritated
visitors and created 'form friction' i.e. the registration form
becomes a barrier.

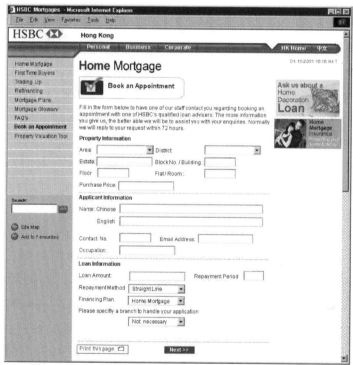

Old enquiry form (17 fields of data) generated two enquiries per week.

The proposed new form with just 3 fields met with initial
internal resistance to this simplification programme which
was based on two factors:

Make an Appointment

We'll be in touch to arrange a date and time convenient for you.

....

I prefer to be contacted by:

○ Phone   ○ Email

Name:

Email Address:

Contact Number :

[Go]

1. It would encourage frivolous and sometimes idiotic enquiries from the likes of Donald Duck and Arnold Schwarzenegger.

2. The old form (with 17 fields) gathered data that integrated well into the existing internal system, i.e. it worked and 'if it ain't broke why fix it?'

The new enquiry form (4fields of data) generated 180 enquiries per week

Yes, the old form (requiring answers to 17 fields) did work or function properly but it also created a major psychological barrier. It drove potential customers away. Most visitors did not have time, nor the inclination to share this amount of personal data at this stage in the buying process.

Not surprisingly, the old form did not generate sufficient enquiries for a business the size of HSBC. After much discussion it was finally agreed to radically change the form and reduce the number of fields from 17 to just 4: Name; email ; Phone Number; Contact preference
Result: New enquiry form generated 180 enquiries per week, boosting revenues from $1m to £20m per quarter (McGovern, 2010).

Small changes can reap big results. But also, small changes can deliver smaller improvements which also really have an impact on the bottom line. Six months of continually finding 0.5% improvement will have a significant impact on your profits. Nurture this culture – the constant beta culture.

Create A Beta Culture

Encourage and insist on split testing emails, ads, web pages, so that you are constantly finding out what works best. Then drop the weakest performing email/ad or web page and run with the the better performing email/ad or web page. This is optimization. Constant small improvements have a big impact on the bottom line.

'Sell something -

get a customer.

Help someone -

get a customer for life.'

(Jay Baer, 2013)

To improve customer service start with morale (culture, motivation, communication), not technology! Interestingly, Netflix 'culture deck' is so important they make it available to anyone on the internet. Although Peter Drucker once said: "Culture eats strategy for breakfast", a flawed strategy will not be saved by an amazing culture. However, you ned to mobilise and motivate your team to execute with passion.

This wonderful Antoine de Saint-Exupery quote is included in Netflix's famous Job Culture Deck (which is available online).

Will an 'A' execution of a 'C' strategy beat a 'C' execution of an "A" strategy

A professor once said: 'An "A" execution of a "C" strategy will beat a "C" execution of an "A" strategy every time.' However, I believe that a lousy ('C') strategy like the Sinclair C5 eCar strategy, kills a product no matter how excellent ('A') the execution. Ideally get both Strategy and Executions (Actions) right = success.

Now let's move to the final section of your plan: Control. Who needs to see what metrics, how often and, most importantly, what do you do if the metrics are up or down?

Chapter 6 Control

SOSTAC® is a registered trade mark of www.PRSmith.org

6.1 Building 'control' into your plan

Your plan needs to include control systems that let you know whether you are on target to achieve the objectives you set earlier. You don't want to wait until the end of the year, when it's too late, to change your tactics. You need early warning systems.

The 'Control' section of your plan lists which KPIs are measured daily and which are measured monthly or quarterly. This section of your plan also specifies who measures what, when and how much it costs. This puts you in control.

All the metrics you measure at the end of each period, will be used in the next period's Situation Analysis when analyzing performance (results).

The 'Performance/results section in the Situation Analysis is then used to inform, or set, more realistic Objectives.

The objectives then need to be controlled, or monitored regularly.

Your plan should specify what will be measured, by whom, when (how frequently), and most importantly, what happens if you are way below or above the target? Your plan may include guidelines about which manager should be alerted if something is not working and also if something is working really well.

Here are the objectives we looked at in the Objectives section. The actual performance is monitored and fed into various types of reporting systems (or dashboards).

6.2 Measuring the KPIs

KPI	Results Previous Period	Objective Current Period	Results Current Period
ROI (Return On Investment)			
Sales - units - value			
Market Share - units - value			
Market Leader Number (in top 5)			
Awareness Level (offline survey)			

Measuring KPIs (contd.)

Preference Level (offline survey)			
NPS Score (Net Promoter Score)			
Sentiment Score (incl. competitor comparison)			

Website/Blog
  Unique Visitors
  Average Duration
  Subscribers to updates/Newsletter
  Leads generated			

Cost Per Visitor (website)			
Cost Per Like (Facebook)			
Cost Per Lead			
Cost Per Customer Acquisition			
Cost Per Customer Retention			
Database Size			
Prospects/Leads			
Customers			
Advocates			
Influencers			

Measuring Website KPIs

KPI	Results Previous Period	Objective Current Period	Results Current Period
Site Visits			
Unique Visitors			
Bounce Rate			
Duration			
Page Views passive engagement			
Most Popular Page(s)			
Most popular downloads			
Engagement - Downloads			
Engagement - Likes/Favorites			
Engagement - Comments			
Engagement - Shares			
Engagement - Registrations/Newsletter			
Churn Rate			
Conversions Leads & Sales			
Sales (all sales)			
Task Completion			

SCAR (Shopping Cart Abandonment Rate)			
Satisfaction Score			
NPS Score			
Sentiment Score			
Share of Voice			

Social Media Platforms – repeat for each platform			
Followers/Likes – engagement etc.			

The anarchy of ignorance

'We prefer the discipline of knowledge
to the anarchy of ignorance.
We pursue knowledge the way a pig pursues truffles.'

David Ogilvy, Ogilvy & Mather, Corporate Culture,
What we believe and how we behave: Nine Obiter Dicta

- You may find it helpful to use the sales funnel to monitor firstly, the number of visitors and
- secondly, the number of visitors becoming prospects (or leads)

as demonstrated by click behaviour (or digital body language) such as filling in a form, or watching all of a product demonstration video reveals a visitor's increased interest (i.e. a prospect or a 'lead'). Prospects become Hot

Prospects (or 'opportunities') by, say, making a second visit, or checking out the feedback/reviews or visiting the pricing page, or filling in the shopping basket (but not purchasing). It is also worth monitoring the percentage of hot prospects converting to sales and eventually converting to repeat sales.

The Sales Funnel

The funnel can be further analyzed so we can see the actual cost per visitor, cost per lead, cost per order and cost per retnetion. There are many different formats for dashboards. The dashboard on the next page is from SmartInsights.

It is used for forecasting (setting objectives) and then subsequently for monitoring / reviewing the actual performance against the objective month-on-month   and year-on-year objective (or target). Since Google Analytics doesn't always give the most practical reporting dashboards, many businesses are now using data visualisation tools such as Google's Data Studio, Microsoft's Power BI and Tableau. These tools enable superior, more professional reports that show the channel and goals deltas (e.g. month-on-month, year-on-year changes) needed to manage performance much more clearly than was practical in Google Analytics.

Another benefit of these tools is that you can use different API data sources to pull in and combine different data. For example search keyword data and Facebook advertising information.

The columns across the top show where traffic is coming from: Advertising (ad network), Search (paid search & natural search), Partners (affiliates, aggregators, sponsorship, email).

Costs and revenues are in the left hand side column: Media Costs (set up/creative, CPM, CPC, Media Costs, Total Costs); Media Impressions & Response (impressions, Click Through Rate, site visits); Conversion To Opportunity/Lead (number of opportunities, cost per opportunity); Conversion to Sales (sales, % of sales & Cost Per Sale); Costs & Profitability are also tracked across every channel.

		Advertising		Search		Partners				All digital media channels
		Ad buys (CPM)	Ad network (CPM)	Paid search (CPC)	Natural search	Affiliates (CPA)	Aggregators (CPA)	Sponsorship (Fixed)	Email list (CPM)	Total or Average
Media costs	Setup/ creative / Mgt costs	£0	£0	£0		£0	£0	£0	£0	£0
	CPM	£10.0	£10.0	£4.0	£1.8	£10.0	£20.0	£100.0	£10.0	£4
	CPC	£5.0	£5.0	£0.20	£0.90	£5.0	£10.0	£33.3	£100.0	£0
	Media costs	£10,000	£10,000	£30,000	£30,000	£10,000	£10,000	£10,000	£10,000	£120,00
	Total cost:setup & media	£10,000	£10,000	£30,000	£30,000	£10,000	£10,000	£10,000	£10,000	£120,00
	Budget %	10%	8%	30%	32%	10%	16%	10%	10%	120
Media impressions & Response	Impressions or names	1,000,000	1,000,000	7,500,000	16,666,667	1,000,000	500,000	100,000	10,000	27,776,9
	CTR	0.2%	0.2%	2.0%	0.2%	0.2%	0.2%	0.3%	1.0%	0.7
	Clicks or site visits	2,000	2,000	150,000	33,333	2,000	1,000	300	100	190,7
Conversion to Opportunity (Lead)	Conversion rate to opportunity	100.0%	100.0%	100.0%	100.0%	100.0%	100.0%	100.0%	100.0%	100.0
	Number of opportunities	2,000	2,000	150,000	33,333	2,000	1,000	300	100	190,7
	Cost per opportunity	£5.0	£5.0	£0.2	£0.9	£5.0	£10.0	£33.3	£100.0	£0
Conversion to Sales	Conversion rate to sale	100.0%	100.0%	100.0%	100.0%	50.0%	100.0%	100.0%	100.0%	93.6
	Number of sales	2,000	2,000	150,000	33,333	1,000	1,000	300	100	189,7
	% of sales	1.1%	1.1%	79.1%	17.6%	0.5%	0.5%	0.2%	0.1%	100.0
	Cost per sale (CPA)	£5.0	£5.0	£0.2	£0.9	£10.0	£10.0	£33.3	£100.0	£0
Revenue	Total revenue	£100,000	£100,000	£7,500,000	£1,666,667	£50,000	£50,000	£15,000	£5,000	£9,486,6
Costs		£70,000	£70,000	£5,250,000	£1,166,667	£35,000	£35,000	£10,500	£3,500	£6,646,6
		£10,000	£10,000	£30,000	£30,000	£10,000	£10,000	£10,000	£10,000	£120,0
		£80,000	£80,000	£5,280,000	£1,196,667	£45,000	£45,000	£20,500	£13,500	£6,760,6
Profitability	Profit	£20,000	£20,000	£2,220,000	£470,000	£5,000	£5,000	-£5,500	-£8,500	£2,726,0
	Return on Investment	25.0%	25.0%	42.0%	39.3%	11.1%	11.1%	-26.8%	-63.0%	40.

This dashboard is from www.SmartInsights.com. The columns and rows are explained above and on the previous page.

Apologies for the tiny print. You can, download your own spreadsheets and templates from Smart Insights (you must register on the site).

Note:
CPM (Cost Per Thousand/Mille reached) and CPC (Cost Per Click) calculated based on total cost for comparison. This is not a full ROI or lifetime value model since future lifetime value is not included. For SEO, the budget is automatically placed into setup/creative costs and you have to estimate the number of clicks this will deliver. For affiliate marketing, work back from Cost Per Sale (CPS) to calculate sales, opportunities and clicks, so changing click-through and conversion rates impacts the cells to the left rather than right.

The blue cells indicate the main control parameters for each media which are important to improving cost effectiveness.

How to use this spreadsheet
First define expected conversion rates to opportunity (lead) and sale for different media (can be set to same value for simplicity).

Then establish realistic costs for purchasing different media (CPM, CPA, CPC) as appropriate for your market. Finally vary the mix of impressions for different media, remembering that there are limits to media that can be purchased (e.g. number of search terms).

Vary the impressions to maximize the number of sales and minimize CPA while also minimizing the risk of purchasing too much of one type of media - a more balanced budget diversifies risk.

To compare the effectiveness of media look at differences in media for CPS and as a percentage of budget and as a percentage of sales.

DISCLAIMER

The previous spreadsheet is provided in good faith for modelling budgets and performance for digital marketing. Smart Insights (Marketing Intelligence) Limited cannot be held responsible for the consequences of any errors in, or misinterpretation of, the spreadsheet models or for any actions taken as a result of using this spreadsheet. Please ask questions or let me know if you believe there are formula errors, so that we can update.

WARNING!

'The single biggest problem in communication
is the illusion that it has taken place.'
George Bernard Shaw.

Yes, this is often the case, but we now have tools to actually check and see if communications are working and how comms affects awareness and behaviour. PR Smith

---

Using spreadsheets and funnels helps you to be in control, see what's working (and then increase this) and see what's not working (modify it, test it or stop it).

But beware of being overwhelmed by information and analytics. Information fatigue syndrome is causing people to become ill as they struggle to manage all the information thrown at them. So be focused about what key information you really need to make better decisions.

Stop wasting time on stuff that doesn't help you
Too much info and not enough action.
'What data is valuable and what data isn't?
Stop wasting time on stuff that doesn't help you.'
Steve Jackson (2011) Cult of Analytics

So, in addition to regularly monitoring dashboards stuffed with metrics, you also need to schedule the following control mechanisms into your plan:

- Website Usability Testing
- Website Satisfaction Monitoring
- Website NPS
- Website Bounce Rate
- Website Traffic Quality
- Which Channels Deliver Best Quality Visitors?
- Social Media Supporting The Brand - Delivering Results?
- Content Marketing Supporting The Brand - Delivering Results?
- Share Of Voice – is it too small?

6.3 Is your website under control?

Does Your Website Work Properly?
Or does it enrage your visitors with dead ends, broken links, error 404s, shopping carts that crash and worse? The Olympics come around every four years and to a particular city every it can be every fifty or a hundred years. London 2012 was a great Olympics but buying tickets on the website proved too difficult for many. After this came the the Glasgow 2014 Commonwealth Games website ticket malfunction resulted in headlines like:

Website fiasco

<u>Sale of Commonwealth Games tickets suspended in website fiasco</u>. The Guardian 14 May 2014
How could this happen again? What kind of web usability testing did they carry out?

Usability Testing

Usability Testing asks various stakeholders to carry out specific tasks whilst being observed, e.g. a journalist is asked to find last month's press release or blog update; an investor is asked to find the annual report; a customer is asked to find product x and buy it etc. This usually identifies any glaring problems with the website.

It's basic stuff but how come the Olympics 2012, Glasgow 2014 and Rugby World Cup websites did not function fully when tickets went on sale? What kind of testing did they run?

Does your website satisfy your visitors?

You can do a separate **'pop up' survey** just as a visitor is leaving your site. Remember to check that the people answering the survey are in your target market group. An exit pop up survey must be short and should be limited to just a handful of questions.

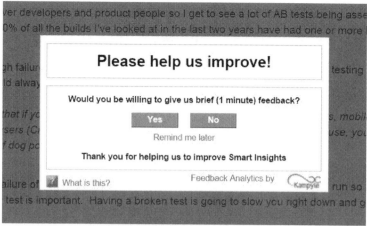

A pop-up survey can reveal critical insights

Does your website generate a positive NPS score?

Or even a one question pop up; 'On a scale of 1-10, how likely are you to recommend this site to someone else? 1 being 'never' and 10 being 'definitely'. This is at the heart of Net Promoter Score (NPS) where you count all the 1-6 scores as negatives and all the 9-10 scores as positive. Ignore 7-8. Then take % of negative score from the % of positive scores to get your NPS.

Any NPS above 0 is considered "good", +50 is "Excellent," and above 70 is considered "world class."

Regardless of the actual score, use NPS scores to continually drive improvements.

Is 88% bounce rate and 1% conversion good or bad?

A bounce rate of 88% and a conversion rate of 1% - is this good or bad?

A bounce rate of 88% means approximately 9/10 visitors don't find your site relevant/interesting and leave it after only visiting one page.

A conversion rate of 1% means that only 1 in 100 sign up or convert. Either we need to improve the site or we are getting the wrong traffic. Find the industry average conversion rate (from Google Analytics benchmarking: Hitwise data). If the industry average is 3% then, yes, 1% conversion is an issue that needs fixing immediately.

You can review and improve engagement rates across different page types since bounce and conversion rate vary a lot depending on the content and design of the particular landing page.

Measure Milliseconds

"Ele.me is the biggest food ordering service in China," Luke Wroblewski wrote in October 2017. Their Progressive Web App gets "skeleton screens up in 400 ms and is fully interactive in 2 seconds." McGovern 2017

400 milliseconds. Digital leaders don't think in seconds. Seconds are so analog. Digital leaders think in milliseconds, milliseconds, milliseconds. Google and Amazon know that customer experience is affected in increments of 100 milliseconds. That's one tenth of a second. Yes, a second, with 90% knocked off. McGovern 2017

Is 96% SCAR (shopping cart abandonment rate) good or bad?

Bad if 50% is the average SCAR from across your industry. Good, or at least marginally better, if 99% is the norm across your industry for the last 6 months!

What actions do you take? Expert walk through Shopping Cart experience? Do an exit survey to find out why?

To improve SCAR requires resources. To get resources you need to tell management about losing £250k pw from SCAR rather than talking about reducing shopping cart abandonment from 96% to 50%.

Remember customers abandoning shopping carts also get annoyed and some of them get angry and vociferous. So, it really is worth analyzing and fixing a high abandonment rate.

Some customers get angry. Although you can't see them online, you can still monitor them (and respond to them online).

Is your traffic under control? - the right visitors - VQVC

Given that there are so many metrics, you might find VQVC a useful reminder of four measures that are worth analyzing: Volume, Quality, Value and Cost. Volume typically measures traffic (unique visitors, visits, page views etc.). Quality measures the quality of the type of visitor (measured by bounce rate, duration, pages per visit). Value measures ultimately £ sales value which a particular campaign might generate by driving a visitor to visit/like/download or even buy when visiting a particular page.

This involves assigning £ value to click behaviour, e.g. Nokia estimated the value of a non-Facebook fan customer was only worth $63 compared to Facebook fan customers at $171; Coca-Cola $120 v $190; Red bull $50 v $113; Nike $83 v $205 (Chaffey & Smith, 2013).

Finally, Costs means calculating the Cost per Acquisition (of a visitor; of a lead; of a sale).

Are your channels under control - multichannel funnels – analytics?

Go back to Situation Analysis, Customer Analysis, 'How do customers buy?' I mentioned Google's Multichannel funnel analysis tools to monitor their online journey, e.g. 'How long do your visitors take to make a purchase? How many channels do your visitors use? etc., since customers generally make more than one visit to a site before buying.

Their multiple visits also often come from many different channels whether a general organic search (via a search engine) or a branded search, a PPC Ad, a link, or by directly inserting the web address into a browser.

Multichannel funnels give marketers more control as they can see which channels are assisting the sales and what the preferred journeys (or combination of channels) are.

This puts marketers in control of their destiny as they can now make informed decisions about where is the optimum channel to spend their resources.

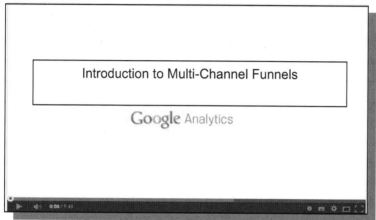

Multi-Channel Funnels Report video is on YouTube

Is your social media under control and always enhancing your brand?

Although we'll dedicate the final section of SOSTAC® to 'control', it is worth mentioning now that without social media guidelines (and for that matter, PR Guidelines) major faux pas (mistakes) occur.

Senior management normally avoid any undesirable press coverage.

Today, as social media makes everyone a 'citizen journalist' a casual comment picked up by someone with a mobile phone can be a source of constant embarrassment.

As Ged Carroll says, 'There is no longer any off the record.' And I'm not talking about former Manchester united, England and QPR former première league fullback,

Rio Ferdinand's irresponsible tweets that brought the game into disrepute, invoked a large fine and a three-match suspension. I'm talking about the chairman of VW making comments about competition within the range of video cameras. See next page for the full story which was caught on video.

No internal marketing (training for all staff) = no control!
Training your staff and issuing social media guidelines not only reduces the risk of major faux pas, but it also helps when you want to spread your marketing content and announcements since your staff can help to seed your content into their own networks (if the staff deem it appropriate – see the social media checklist in the Actions section that increases the likelihood that your staff will like it and share it).

A Social Media Disaster Story

At the Frankfurt Motor Show in 2011 Volkswagen Chairman Martin Winterkorn was filmed admiring the Hyundai i30 model. In particular, he noticed the lack of noise on the adjustable steering wheel.

As he spoke to his chief designer, his embarrassing comments were recorded to create a video much cited by his South Korean rivals.

VW chairman caught on camera on YouTube commenting on
Competition at the 2011 Frankfurt Motor Show

"Why can they do it? BMW cannot do it, we cannot do
it" said the unguarded VW chairman. (Foy, 2014). Over
2m people have watched this video on YouTube alone.

6.3 Is your marketing content under control?

Whether you are producing a book, ebook, video,
instagrams, blog posts, tweets (remember the content
pyramid in the action section), you need to think about
controlling content metric goals.

This means that equipped with a clearly defined audience
and clearly defined goals, you brainstorm, select and
produce content.

If the goal is to generate conversions to newsletter
registration and eventually conversion to revenue, then
make sure your content has a direct way to make this
happen, i.e. add direct links to these landing pages so it
becomes easy to measure the effectiveness of your content.

Watch this 25 minute video about 'How To Measure The
Effectiveness Of Content Marketing' (courtesy of Steve
Farnsworth and Erin Robbins), on prsmith.org/blog. It
really puts marketing content and analytics together very
nicely.

Erin Robbins on the Effectiveness Of
Content Marketing prsmith.org/blog

6.4 Is your share of voice under control?

In this case, 'Share of Voice' is the percentage of all online
content and conversations about your company, or your
brand, compared to your competitors. Do you have a
presence in important conversations? What about
competition?

Then you start asking if you should increase or reduce your
presence? Are people making positive or negative
comments about your company or brand? How quickly do
you respond (if at all)? Do the responses satisfy those
making the comments? If you don't know or can't see what
your target market is saying about you on a quantitative,

qualitative, and tonal basis, then you are 'marketing in the dark with a blindfold on' (Cramer, 2014). It is simply essential to see what is being said about you. There is no choice here.

Word-of-mouth brings us back to the old PR days when agencies would gather the newspapers and magazines (and check TV and radio) and count how many mentions the brand got (compared to the competition) and later they scored them either positive or negative according to good and bad mentions. After that came a single score.

Today we call it **sentiment analysis**. Since all media has fragmented into smaller, better-targeted media including blogs, Facebook and Twitter streams, then there are a lot more people publishing their 'voice'. You also need to listen to what is being said about your competitors (and your own business). Hence, Sentiment Analysis has become popular – with some boards of directors wanting to see the sentiment score reported regularly.

As well as Search Engine Share Of Voice, there is also Advertising Share Of Voice. You can see more in Appendix 8.

What information do I need to make a great decision?

Turn information into action. Use information to make better decisions. Ask yourself 'what information do I need to make a great decision?'

6.5 Can you double sales with exit polls?

Say 20% of your visitors stay on your site long enough (or return several times) and watch the product video, look at the customer reviews, check out the prices but most of them don't convert. According to their digital body language or click behavior, these visitors are qualified leads (they are seriously interested in your product/service.

Say 2 % of your visitors convert. That means 18% of your qualified leads don't buy. You need to know why not. A simple pop-up exit survey can help to double your sales. Q1 What were you looking to do today on our site (a) find a product (b) check prices (c) check reviews (d) other (state) Q2 Did you achieve your goal today? [ ] Yes [ ] No Q3 How can we help you better?

If this information allowed you to find a solution and offer it to these non converters, you might get say 10% of the hot prospects/non converters to convert. 10% of 18% (of non converters) = 1.8% or let's round it up to 2% extra sales conversions. Add this to your original 2% conversion rate and voila, you have doubled sales.

**Using real time analytics to make better
real time marketing mix decisions**

So here's what 1-800-FLOWERS.COM (working with SAS) now do – they quickly spot issues and remedy them. What if a fulfilment florist in a certain ZIP code delivers late or has to substitute inferior flowers?

They can now see complaints and low scores in real time and automatically adjust orders sent to the distributor florist

---

based on consumer concerns.

They also adjust the product mix offered on the Website. If too many florists are struggling to get a certain kind of tulip called for in a particular bouquet (and thus customers complain about substitutions), 1-800-FLOWERS.COM can quickly spot this trend and remove the bouquet from its Website temporarily (if it's just a temporary shortage) or permanently if necessary.

They estimate that this has improved its enterprise customer service value ratio by 100 basis points, which translates to millions in revenue.

Desai, N. Making customer connections bloom, Saas Customer Stories

6.6 Constant learnings and insights

In addition to presenting their KPIs at the end of the year Procter & Gamble ask their managers to present up to seven 'learnings' or insights that they've gleaned from their marketplace. Here are two examples from Smart Insights Party case:

(1) Google Analytics reveals Pinterest impact on sales
GA shows that Pinterest drives an average of 1,000 new sales to our website each month. Whilst this is relatively low, these are higher spending visitors with an average spend of £140. They particularly buy the 'party packs' and 25% of them opt for the express delivery service.

(2) Customer research reveals preference for images vs discount stories

Our website includes a space where our visitors can share their purchase with friends. Less than 0.5% do so. Customer **research has revealed that this is because customers did not want to admit to 'having spent only £15 on a knockout necklace'.** So rather than sharing purchase information, we'll ask customers to share images of the product and/or images wearing the jewellery on the website, Facebook, Twitter and Pinterest. We know that when images are shared, sales are generated. Clickthrough to sale from an image is 0.5%. Therefore the more images that are available and the more that the images are shared, the more sales increase.

Your analytics can reveal some real insights about customers. This and all other KPIs can be subsequently used in the next 'Situation Analysis'.

Marketers often measure the wrong things

Like satisfaction (product/service satisfaction), engagement, interaction, relationships, loyalty. So much marketing and branding hyperbole. What are they missing?

"We don't always want to engage. We don't always want an experience. Sometimes, we just want to get things done as quickly and easily as possible." Gerry McGovern

So why is usability so often ignored?

'Amazon has known for a long time that the further away they pushed the login process the more they sold. If you make it simpler, people buy more. If you make it simpler, people stay with you longer. Reducing hassle increases sales.' (Gerry McGovern, 2014). Do we measure this 'reducing hassle'?

Monitoring and measurement can motivate staff

Earnestly monitoring KPIs to identify problems earlier rather than later, so your team can make changes to ensure they hit their targets. Rewards for achieving KPIs (need to think this through carefully – as people will expect it after a while).

Non-financial rewards, e.g. gifts (which are also called 'psychic income' if the gifts appeal to their higher-level needs of being loved, self-esteem and self-realization) can be much more motivating (and sometimes cost less if you get trade prices or bulk discounts!)

Monitoring and measuring stops wasting money

Having good control systems in place reveals what works well (and therefore do more of this sooner rather than later) and also shows what isn't working so well.

Good monitoring systems stop money from being wasted and ensure that money spent is constantly optimized.

Good control system stop money being wasted

6.7 Constant Analysis for 'Always On'

We talked about the need for an 'Always On' approach in Chapter 4, Tactics. This requires constant analysis to ensure we do more of what works and less of what doesn't. You need to schedule time each month (or week) to test-learn-refine so that you are constantly optimising.

6.8 90 Day Planning

90 day planning can help ensure your plan delivers the right results. A quarterly or 90-day focus helps to break down the annual plan into manageable parts which are then broken down by month and week.

KPI	Jan	Feb	Mar	Q1 Total
Site Visitors	10,000	10,000	10,000	30,000
Leads	1,000	1,000	1,000	1,000
Total Units	100	100	100	300
Total ASP	£10	£10	£10	£10
Total revenue	£1,000	£1,000	£1,000	£3,000

Monitoring KPIs does not always have to involve a lot of manual spreadsheet work; you can use APIs and feeds to automate the preparation of these results tables (e.g. using the Google Analytics API).

90-day plans should include:
KPIs for the 90 days broken down by month
Key milestones for tactics (e.g. launch new content – Best Practice Guide)

Deliverables required to ensure tactics are delivered on time
Launch new Best Practice Guide

Deliverable	Status	Owner	Deadline
Copy Created	Green	Jim	10 Jan
Visuals sources	Green	Ali	20 Jan
Guide produced	Green	Mel	22 Jan
Influencers contacted	Orange	Ali	22 Jan
eMail created	Orange	Jim	25 Jan
News releases created	Red	Phil	31 Jan

Red = Deliverable is not on track and unlikely to be delivered on time
Amber = Risky, identify underlying problems and address them
Green= on track

You can see how the Control and Action sections can overlap. That's absolutely fine because as long as you include all the elements of SOSTAC®, you will have the foundation for a perfect plan whichever particular final format you decide.

Summary

So this is SOSTAC®. Don't forget to add in your 3Ms, the 3 key resources: Men and Women, Money (budgets) & Minutes (timescales).

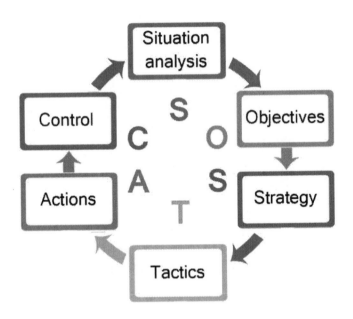

+3Ms (The 3 Key Resources)

Men and Women

The human resource. Skilled marketers will be in demand and particularly during this period of radical change to marketing. Here's another possible marketing team: Digital Marketing Specialist; Designer (Customer Journey Designer); Social Media Manager; Chief Listening Officer; Content Marketing (including Blogger); SEO Specialist; App Designer; App Developer; Cloud Services Specialist; Big Data Analyst; Market Research Data Miner, Data Officer (GDPR); AI Service Leader. If you cannot recruit, train and motivate internally, can you find the people externally in agencies with the right skill sets?

Money

Budgets – you need budgets. Whether 5% of forecasted sales if you are B2C or 1-2% if B2B (up to 8 times higher if it is a new product or service being launched), this percentage of forecasted sales is a common benchmark. However, increasingly marketers will be asked to justify why they need their budgets – reverting to the ideal approach or task approach.

Minutes

Time is often the most limited resource. Particularly when you define what information you need to make a great decision but discover you haven't got the time to collect the information. Add in A/B testing and pilot testing and you'll see why time is at a premium. Incidentally, perhaps it's time to stop thinking about campaigns and start thinking about conversations (and constant beta/constant improvement).

Blend Analytics, Engineering and Creativity

'To stay ahead or be a part of this digital upheaval, brands must adopt a hacker mind-set of testing, iterating and improving by blending analytics, engineering and creativity.' (Hudson, 2014).

I hope this SOSTAC® guide has been useful to you, triggered some ideas, helped you to structure your plan or even adopt and integrate it with any other planning structure that you might prefer.

You can see more applications of SOSTAC® Plannng framework in the SOSTAC® Portal www.SOSTAC.org . Having absorbed all the information in this book, you are ready to use your knowledge in an online open-book, 1 hour, multiple choice, SOSTAC® mini case study and become a SOSTAC® Certified Planner. There are two manuals (some of which overlap with this book) and some examples of SOSTAC® plans.

Visit www.SOSTAC.org and become a SOSTAC® Certified Planner.

I wish you well with your plans. Keep perfecting them.

Paul
PR Smith

PS Finally, here is a summary infographic of SOSTAC® followed by a challenging, manifesto for businesses going forward – Mark Schaefer's Human Manifesto.

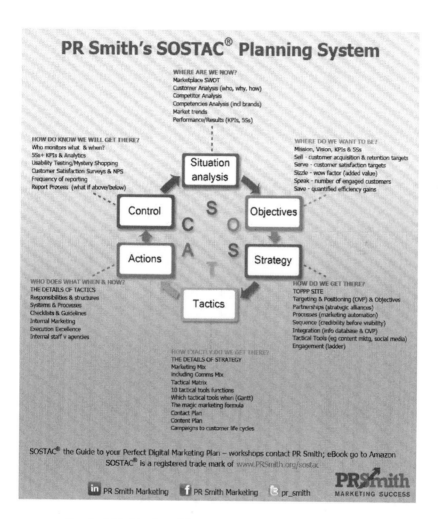

PR Smith's SOSTAC® Planning System

WHERE ARE WE NOW?
Marketplace SWOT
Customer Analysis (who, why, how)
Competitor Analysis
Competencies Analysis (incl brands)
Market trends
Performance/Results (KPIs, 5Ss)

HOW DO KNOW WE WILL GET THERE?
Who monitors what & when?
5Ss+ KPIs & Analytics
Usability Testing/Mystery Shopping
Customer Satisfaction Surveys & NPS
Frequency of reporting
Report Process (what if above/below)

WHERE DO WE WANT TO BE?
Mission, Vision, KPIs & 5Ss
Sell - customer acquisition & retention targets
Serve - customer satisfaction targets
Sizzle - wow factor (added value)
Speak - number of engaged customers
Save - quantified efficiency gains

Situation analysis — Control — Objectives — Actions — Strategy — Tactics

S O S T A C

WHO DOES WHAT WHEN & HOW?
THE DETAILS OF TACTICS
Responsibilities & structures
Systems & Processes
Checklists & Guidelines
Internal Marketing
Execution Excellence
Internal staff v agencies

HOW DO WE GET THERE?
TOPPP SITE
Targeting & Positioning (OVP) & Objectives
Partnerships (strategic alliances)
Processes (marketing automation)
Sequence (credibility before visibility)
Integration (info database & OVP)
Tactical Tools (eg content mktg, social media)
Engagement (ladder)

HOW EXACTLY DO WE GET THERE?
THE DETAILS OF STRATEGY
Marketing Mix
Including Comms Mix
Tactical Matrix
10 tactical tools functions
Which tactical tools when (Gantt)
The magic marketing formula
Contact Plan
Content Plan
Campaigns to customer life cycles

SOSTAC® the Guide to your Perfect Digital Marketing Plan – workshops contact PR Smith; eBook go to Amazon
SOSTAC® is a registered trade mark of www.PRSmith.org/sostac

in PR Smith Marketing   f PR Smith Marketing   pr_smith   **PRSmith** MARKETING SUCCESS

Download this &/or the mobile version from prsmith.org/SOSTAC

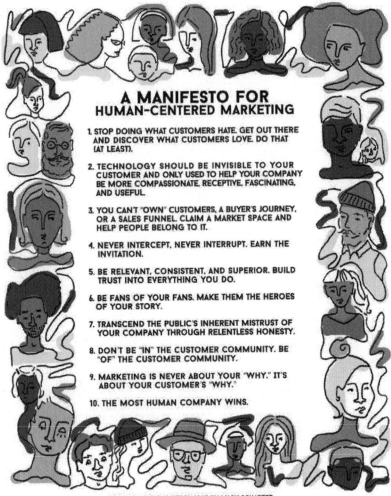

A MANIFESTO FOR HUMAN-CENTERED MARKETING

1. STOP DOING WHAT CUSTOMERS HATE. GET OUT THERE AND DISCOVER WHAT CUSTOMERS LOVE. DO THAT (AT LEAST).

2. TECHNOLOGY SHOULD BE INVISIBLE TO YOUR CUSTOMER AND ONLY USED TO HELP YOUR COMPANY BE MORE COMPASSIONATE, RECEPTIVE, FASCINATING, AND USEFUL.

3. YOU CAN'T "OWN" CUSTOMERS, A BUYER'S JOURNEY, OR A SALES FUNNEL. CLAIM A MARKET SPACE AND HELP PEOPLE BELONG TO IT.

4. NEVER INTERCEPT, NEVER INTERRUPT. EARN THE INVITATION.

5. BE RELEVANT, CONSISTENT, AND SUPERIOR. BUILD TRUST INTO EVERYTHING YOU DO.

6. BE FANS OF YOUR FANS. MAKE THEM THE HEROES OF YOUR STORY.

7. TRANSCEND THE PUBLIC'S INHERENT MISTRUST OF YOUR COMPANY THROUGH RELENTLESS HONESTY.

8. DON'T BE "IN" THE CUSTOMER COMMUNITY. BE "OF" THE CUSTOMER COMMUNITY.

9. MARKETING IS NEVER ABOUT YOUR "WHY." IT'S ABOUT YOUR CUSTOMER'S "WHY."

10. THE MOST HUMAN COMPANY WINS.

FROM "MARKETING REBELLION" BY MARK SCHAEFER

Reproduced by kind permission of mark Schaefer, author Marketing Rebellion (2019).

Appendices

Appendix 1.1: A Persona Called Tapio

Here is a completed persona for Tapio who is a 36 year old Finnish entrepreneur working for himself. Often working on the road, in the office or from home, Tapio has a variety of different needs from his broadband and his mobile service provider. He needs primarily to be able to check email, store contacts and easily upload and download files through secure networks. His wife would also need a good home internet connection for her own home/office lifestyle, having even more need for the ability to upload and download large files. He is in the market for his own broadband connection and mobile phone contract.

Products: Broadband Internet Connection; Mobile phone contract. Meet Tapio……..

Goals	Purchase broadband connection for home use
Scenario	Tapio has decided he needs to get a broadband connection for his own personal home use. He has just moved apartment and needs a new service. He and his wife both know through word of mouth that they are in a buyer's market and will use the internet to find the best deal they can. Also through word of mouth Tapio heard technical details that 100Mb was a fast broadband connection. Tapio knows all the major brands via offline branding campaigns such as TV, billboards and stickers on the sides of public transport vehicles.
Tasks prior to pur- chase	Check brand websites directly. Compare brand prices (Google). Compare full service offers (Google). Figure out if 100Mb is what he needs to run a good connection from home Learn how to install the system
Consid- erations and questions	There are a variety of broadband deals in Finland so it is important to find out what the brands offer. What is the price per month? How many service/price (speed to Mb ratio) options are there and are they understandable? Does the cost vary based on usage? If so, how? If not, is the price fixed or could there be hidden surprises? Tapio's wife doesn't want to use cables to connect to the Internet. Is the broadband connection wireless? Does this cost more? Do any free accessories (i.e. wireless modem) come with the service?

	Are there any free offers in Finland around broadband? If so, are the free offers comparable in terms of features? Tapio heard that a full system contract including digital TV could be purchased with broadband access to the Internet? Is this possible in his location? Does the system come home-fitted? Is it manual installation? If so is it easy? Are there service guarantees? Money back options or trial periods?
Pain points	Neither Tapio nor his wife have any idea how to install broadband and don't know anything about the technology. Tapio heard he needed a 100Mb connection because it's fast but doesn't know how much benefit he will get for the extra money.
Search terms	Finnish terms (same in English); Laajakaista (broadband) Laajakaista Yhteys (broadband connection) Laajakaista Nopeus (broadband fast/speed) Laajakaista Hinnat (broadband prices)
Key paths/ content	Look on the website that Tapio will use for the information that answers all his considerations/questions.

Appendix 1.2: Personas with customer journeys

Persona	Name	Robert		Personal and home	Lives in Boulder, CO
	Type	Primary persona			Keen snowboarder and ultra-runner in summer
	Decision role	Main decision maker in startup			Married for 5 years
Demographics	Age	35 y.o.		Work	CTO responsible for service availability
	Gender	Male			Online Diet service / startup
	Buying unit	Reports to COO, CFO and CEO			Serving consumers
Decision making	Style	Product evaluation style			12 people in development, design and infrastructure
		5 month timescale to deployment			

Goals and motivations	• Demand spikes are jeopardising the growth of the business • Wants to focus on core competencies - developing customer proposition • Looking to reduce costs and internal admin time	Buying scenario	Robert is seeking a managed cloud (Infrastructure as a Service, IaaS) to scale virtual server space, processors, bandwidth and load balancers Has to make business case to 3 more senior colleagues Since launch 2 years ago the company has seen rapid growth with a 50X revenue growth in the previous year involving 300K average daily site visits with spikes up to one million daily uniques requiring IaaS Previously had a part time system admin responsible for up-time
Barriers and Challenges	• New year spikes are literally keeping Robert awake at night • Needs 50+ web servers, multiple database servers and load balancer • Want to support 10 million uniques maximum per day • Only 5 months to deploy before Christmas spike • Not sure about using a third party or direct to AWS, Azure		
Our key messages	• Speed to market • Flexibility to grow with you • Your dedicated support team	Preferred media	Work: CIO.com, Quora, Stackexchange for queries Home: Medium blogs, Boarding and Ultra magazines
		Social media use	Work: Twitter (for keeping informed); LinkedIn (for career) Home: Facebook and Instagram (daily)
		Devices	Macbook Pro Latest iPhone

Customer journey map

	Stage 1: Awareness (Discover)	Stage 2: Evaluation (Compare)	Stage 3: Decision (select)
Media touchpoints	Google Quora CIO.com	Clouds360.com G2Crowd.com Itadvisory.com	G2Crowd.com Brand searches
Key questions	Cost savings for business case Time to implement? Potential risks	Independent service quality assessments? Implementation project tasks Cost breakdown	What happens when there is downtime? How do I escalate? How is agreement purchased?
Searches	IaaS Benefits and risks Cloud-based servers Virtual servers and load balancers	Top IaaS providers Managed cloud providers Support quality IaaS	IaaS reviews Azure vs Amazon Web Service Pricing Azure vs AWS
Key content (Types and formats)	Proof points - speed to market Benefits of managed cloud (top-level video and whitepaper) Process of migration	Gartner magic quadrant Service levels Implementation case studies/success stories Why 'company name'	Detailed service level agreement How it works - dedicated support contact Details of team certifications for AWS Options when major problem/deadline?
Interactive tools	Cost savings calculator	Webinar on how to choose a cloud service	Video case study of onboarding

Reproduced by kind permission of Smart Insights – members can access a B2B and B2C example in Excel Format

Appendix 2: Scenario Plan: Nat Semi-Conductor

Like personas, Scenario Planning keeps your copy writers and web designers grounded in the world inhabited by the user'. This example is, arguably, the most potent use of scenario planning is it boosted sales and loyalty and created long term sustainable competitive advantage.

This example actually uses the customer analysis strategically to develop a UX (User Experience) that engages, satisfies and wows customers. This proves Drucker was right – you are only in business for one reason: 'to help your customers'. Sit back and enjoy this exceptional piece of marketing.

NSC supply analogue and digital microchips that process sounds and images for mobiles and DVDs. Target DMU: Design Engineers and Corporate Purchasing Agents (they don't buy but the choices they make/specify at beginning of NPD determine the components bought later). The website gave information about products.

How can the website help engineers?

Launched a project to develop a deep understanding of engineers… including how they work. This helped them learn how they design components. This led them to consider creating online tools (on the website) to help engineers.

Focused on 'power supplies'.

Design engineers under time pressure.
Easy to use tools could speed design process and save time.

Put a multi-functional team together.
Marketing, application designers, web designers, engineers…

Customers work process – identify a design engineer's work process.
Create a part 2. Create a design 3. Analyze the design (simulations)
 2. Build a prototype

Created an online tool web based tool called 'web-bench'
Engineers complete the whole design process without special software. Engineer logs on – he is prompted to specify overall parameter and key components.

Web bench auto-generates possible designs and complete technical specs;

Part lists; prices; and cost benefit analysis.

Engineer then refines the design. Runs real time simulation (using sophisticated that Nat. Semi had licensed and offers it on its site).

Engineer can then alter the design many times.
Save iterations in my portfolio.

Email link to colleagues so they can run and save simulations.

Once engineer agrees the final design, system generates a bill of materials for the prototype c/w Nat Semi's components and all requirements from other manufacturers' c/w links to distributors and prices.

Result: Do in 2 hours what previously took months.
Design engineers loved it.
Designed more than 20,000 power supplies in the first year of operation.

What next? Asked engineers about other activities they had difficulty with. Thermal simulations and circuitry ... new scenarios for engineers who design wireless devices... created web therm... end of year 31,000 visitors on site... 3,000 orders or referrals every day. One integrated socket = 40m units with Nokia. This was 10+ years ago!

Source: Seybold P (2001) Get Inside the Lives of your customers.   HBR May

Note: This was approximately twenty years ago.
National Semi-conductor are now owned by Texas Instruments

Appendix 3: KPMG Visitors' Click Behaviour

Website traffic provides a wealth of information that can, and should, be used in the Situation Analysis as it reveals what stage in the buying process various visitors are and it highlights any visitors who are hot prospects deserving special attention. So here are some additional insights into how KPMG use digital body language (click behaviour) to segment or categorise their visitors to identify how they can help them.

Type	Description	Identification
Prospect	A visitor who submits an RFP or an email to a partner.	A visit that includes an RFP submission or an email to a partner.
Participant	A visitor who registers for an event, the site or content.	A visit that includes a submission of a registration form.
Passive Browser	A visitor who downloads single articles, papers, starts but doesn't finish a video.	A visit that includes a single page view or download, or video view.
Researcher	A visitor who downloads multiple articles, papers, starts and completes more than one video in multiple practice areas or industries.	A visit that includes downloading multiple articles, papers, video start/complete.
Advocate	A visitor who reads an article or paper, or views a video and shares it.	A visit that includes content consumption and sharing of that content.

Type	Description	Identification
Focused Seeker	A visitor who reads multiple content items within a practice area or industry.	A visit that includes multiple touches of content with a practice area or industry section. This visit segment may be used in conjunction with any of the previous segments.
Passive Job Seeker	A visitor who reads content on the Jobs section of the site.	A visit that includes one view of the site content and then leaves the site.
Engaged Job Seeker	A visitor who submits a job search query and views Job Details.	A visit that includes at least one job search query and view of Job Details page.
Participating Job Seeker	A visitor that submits their résumé.	A visit that includes submission of at least one résumé on a Job Details page.
Brand Aware Visitor – First Time and Repeat	A visitor that comes to the site directly.	A visit that begins through a bookmark or direct input of a global or local KPMG URL.

Type	Description	Identification
Responder	A visitor who responds to a KPMG email campaign, or clicks on a link within an alert or newsletter.	A visit that originates with a referral from a link to KPMG web content through a KPMG sourced communication.
Brand Aware Searcher	A visitor who comes to KPMG website through branded SEO, PPC, display ads on third party sites.	A visit that originates with a referral from a link to KPMG web content through a search engine, display ad, or other media where KPMG brand is evident.
Non-Brand Aware Searcher	A visitor who comes to KPMG website through non-branded SEO or PPC.	A visit that originates with a referral from a link to KPMG web content through a search engine.
Passive Social Visitor	A visitor that comes from a social media property (Facebook, Twitter, YouTube) one time.	A visit that originates as a referral from a social media property.
Engaged Social Visitor	A visitor that comes from a social media property (Facebook, Twitter, YouTube) and conducts one of the Engagement actions described in the Metrics Taxonomy.	A visit that originates as a referral from a social media property and ends with the described Engagement task.

Source: KPMG - Reproduced with kind permission

Appendix 4: Different CX on Mobile

Here's a very nicely written two parts from Goldberg (2013), Marketing on Mobile: Why is this Platform Different?

Part 1: So write content differently.
As more and more people adopt smartphones, B2B content marketers are thinking about how to bring their content to mobile users. It's no wonder. comScore, Inc., a leader in measuring the digital world, reported that 55 percent of mobile users in the U.S., 129.4 million people, owned smartphones during the three months ending in January 2013 — a seven percent increase since October.
But clearly, you can't simply take your existing marketing content and move it to a mobile device. You need to create new content in a format best suited to the strengths and limitations of this medium.

In this two-part series on writing content for mobile devices, I'll talk first about why the experience of reading content is different on mobile. In part two, I'll discuss ways to write content to better suit mobile devices.

Why is mobile different?
When you do any type of writing, it's always a good idea to put yourself in the shoes of your reader. The experience of reading on a mobile device is different than reading on a standard desktop, laptop or tablet for three reasons:
Constant interruption. When you're at a computer, people are more likely to assume you're working and leave you alone. If you're looking at a smartphone in a room filled with people, there's a greater chance you'll be interrupted.
Multitasking. There's a much greater chance your reader is multitasking with their smartphone. For example, a dad might be looking up football scores on his smartphone

while waiting for his daughter's chorus performance to begin; a manager may check for text messages or emails while waiting online at the Starbucks drive-through.
Small screen size. The most significant difference between desktop machines and smartphones is the size of the screen. Looking at a smaller screen is more likely to cause eye strain. More importantly, it's harder to retain information and comprehension is lower on these screens.

Why small screens reduce comprehension

According to research presented in the book "Mobile Usability" by Jakob Nielsen and Raluca Budiu, it's 108% more difficult to understand information when reading from a mobile screen compared to reading on a desktop screen. Comprehension suffers for two reasons:
Less visible context. The less you can see, the more you have to remember when you're trying to understand anything that's not fully explained within the viewable space. Because human short-term memory is notoriously weak, less context translates into lower comprehension.
More scrolling. Mobile users have to scroll around more to see other parts of the content rather than simply glancing at the text. Scrolling takes more time, which degrades memory. It also diverts attention from the problem at hand to locating the appropriate part of the page. Additionally, you need to find your previous place on the page.
In the second part of this series, I'll present ways to write content to address these issues.

What other factors contribute to a mobile screen making content marketing more challenging on a mobile device?

Part 2: How to write content for mobile devices

In part one of this two-part series, I talked about why your marketing content needs to be different on mobile devices. In this second part, I address how to write content that will be effective on these devices.

As I mentioned last time, the experience of reading on mobile devices is different from that of a desktop, laptop, or tablet device for three reasons: mobile users are more likely to be interrupted, they're more likely to be multitasking, and the small screen size means that reading comprehension plummets.

So how do you create content that will have an impact under these circumstances? First, consider the types of content that will be most compelling to smartphone users.

You can always ask people what they want. But as a rule of thumb, some types of content that are better suited to mobile include non-editorial content, such as data or an app like a specialty calculator. In terms of written content, start with news content or any content that's constantly updated.

Next, when you write your content, follow these 9 tips:

Less is best. Use shorter sentences. Get rid of any unnecessary words or images. Avoid long pages that require a lot of scrolling.

Get to the point fast. State the most useful, relevant information at the start.

Do one thing at a time. Put only one idea on each page. **State clear goals.** Make clear what action you'd like the reader to take - whether that's sharing your content or signing up for your mailing list.

Make text scannable. Break up text into small chunks or paragraphs. This will add white space between text, making it easier to read and scan. Bulleted lists will make information even more scannable.

Grab the reader. Use sensory words, such as feel, savor, scent, that paint a vivid picture in the reader's mind.

Use contractions and abbreviations.

Summarize. When presenting longer pieces, create an executive summary of the content with a link that they can read later on a tablet, laptop or PDF.

Think multiple platforms. Make it easy to move content cross-platform. For example, by adding a prominent "email this" link.

Cheryl Goldber, C (2013) Marketing on Mobile: Why is this Platform Different? High Tech Communicator, 3 June

Appendix 5: New Ways To Know Your Customer

How cookies, digital body language, big data and marketing automation help you to know your customer

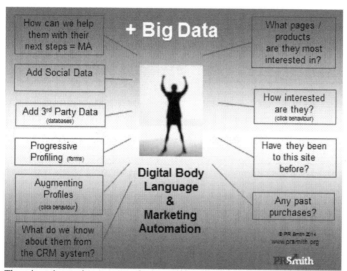

There is an increasing amount of customer data available

A Cookie

Is a small bit of code which is lodged on a visitor's own browser once they visit a site (after asking the visitor's permission). Visitors can delete cookies anytime. It can contain visitor preferences, language preferences, or display settings, past interactions plus any other information that the website has but more often than not, this data will be held separately in a marketing database with the cookie being a user identification which acts as a key to access the rich data collected about a visitor (or customer). A cookie looks like this: User ID A9A3BECE0563982D

The click behaviour (what they click on) is recorded and tells us what pages they looked at, how long they spent looking at them, and if they've been to the site before. It can also link to the marketing database and can see whether the visitor has bought from us before, plus any issues identified in the CRM system such as 'Salesforce'.

On-Site Behaviour (or click behaviour) is recorded. This tells us what products a customer is interested in (duration plus if they've looked at the product video etc.). Click behaviour is digital body language. It identifies how interested a visitor is, e.g. if they leave ('bounce') after a few seconds they get a very low score. If they stay over, say, 5 minutes, look at a product page, watch a product video, download the product spec and add the product to their shopping basket, they get a much higher score as they are a hot prospect. This process of scoring visitors is based around sets of rules.

More advanced marketers (and automated marketing systems) synchronize past purchases with repeat buying patterns and also with click behaviour and automate highly relevant messages to the visitor whether via a tailored landing page, a tailored email, SMS, pop-up page or even snail mail or a phone call from customer service or a sales rep.

Augmenting customer profiles
Is done by analyzing the digital body language or click behavior of a visitor. Click behaviour can include additional activity on the website such as downloading a white paper, watching a video and also non-web behaviour such as opening (or not opening) an email. A score can also integrate purchase of other products.

Progressive profiling

PP Continually collects new information about the visitor by asking just a few new questions on each visit. For example a visitor has already volunteered their name, email and company name. On the next visit they might be asked just one question such as, 'What prompted you to visit us?' or 'Where did you first hear about us?' This data is collected via web forms which essentially add a new field(s) of data to the visitor profile. A visitor is never asked the same question twice. They will never be plagued by unnecessary repeat questions which irritate visitors significantly.

Pulling social data

This means that advanced marketing automation systems can pull or collect publicly available information from a prospect's (or customer's) social media platforms including age, gender, geography (and sometimes email address) and also deeper psychographic information such as interests and groups, hobbies, marital status, political views and friends. Comments posted/shared/liked and reviews written also present an opportunity to build a deeper more comprehensive customer profile. Logging into a website via Social Sign-On (using any of your social media passwords and names) usually gives the website owner access to a visitor's or customer's social information.

Adding third party data

Some marketing automations systems integrate with third party databases such as Dun & Bradstreet B2B databases and directories. Each new sign-up (captured in a web form) triggers an automatic check against a database (e.g. 'we see John Smith from Company XYZ checking to see if he is listed in this directory) to find, and add, a company name, website, address, telephone number (and other company information). See how a train company targets ideal prospect frequent flyers using this system.

This Is Big Data

Big Data refers to large amounts of structured and unstructured data that requires machine-based systems and technologies to create, collect and analyze. Data is everywhere. So too is Big Data and more and more are starting to use it cleverly. From supermarkets, to Lady Gaga, to Google cars to politicians, to the FBI, to children's hospitals to detect infections before they 'occur'; the list goes on.

Clustering, segmenting and profiling

Some systems will analyze a vast amount of data to see if there are any common profiles that relate to their customers (or maybe just amongst their highest spending customers). Once they have a profile they can search for other prospects with similar profiles – sometimes by using more third party databases.

Appendix 6: Blue Ocean Strategy

Blue Ocean Strategy was created by Professors W.Chan Kim and Renée Mauborgne and effectively provides a 'systematic approach to making competition irrelevant and creating uncontested market space'.

Companies competing in the marketplace try to avoid the concept of 'Strategic-Hell', which occurs when it is difficult to find differentiation from competitors and price wars are unavoidable, resulting in diminishing margins, until someone gets squeezed out of the market. Blue Ocean Strategy tries to migrate from those markets and create new ones where pressure from competitors is low or non-existent. For example, Apple iPhones and Apple iPods created new product-markets away from traditional competition.

The concept is appealing but in reality it is difficult to do. Companies need to make a constant effort to imagine how their competitive position could be improved. Blue Ocean's 'four actions' framework may help to achieve the desired position by exploring these four points: 'Eliminated', 'Reduced', 'Raised' and 'Created'. We will use the Cirque du Soleil ('Circus of the Sun' is a dramatic mix of circus arts and street entertainment).

ELIMINATED: Which of the factors that the industry takes for granted should be eliminated? Cirque du Soleil eliminated traditional circus themes, animals.

REDUCED: Which factors should be reduced well below the industry's standard? Cirque du Soleil reduced children focus.

RAISED: Which factors should be raised well above the industry's standard? Cirque du Soleil raised the adult focus (including corporate targeting).

CREATED: Which factors should be created that the industry has never offered? Created multiple productions and artistic dance.

Appendix 7: House of Quality Analysis

The house of quality is a popular name given to the Quality Function Deployment (QFD) diagram created by Yoji Akao, (1966). It is also known as 'the voice of the customer' since the purpose of the analysis is to understand why customers buy (or don't buy) a particular product or service.

The method tries to identify WHAT the customer wants or needs, and HOW it can be delivered (product/service). The WHAT is the market requirement, with the HOW being the design characteristics of the product or service.

This tool may be used as a link between the SITUATION Analysis Section and the Strategy section of SOSTAC®. Once all of the Situation Analysis is complete it is easier to see the Key Success Factors (the market requirements, the WHAT) and the Competitive Distinctive Capabilities (the HOW). The WHAT and the HOW must fit together neatly.

Consider Kodak. Customers want to take pictures (WHAT) and Kodak knows HOW (cameras). WHAT and HOW fit. Then suddenly (and disruptively), digital cameras (a substitute for film) were launched by new competitors and were rapidly adopted by customers. The new WHAT doesn't fit with the traditional KODAK's HOW. Kodak must find a new HOW (new product/service).

If Kodak's What and How fit, the company can build on this. If they do not fit, strategic changes must be made to make them fit. Kodak needed to create a new product or service which fitted with customers WANTs, i.e. ink, printing service, printers, corporate printers, outsourcing printing services and even digital cameras.

These are strategic issues. If no correct strategic solution is found, all the tactics will be wrong regardless (since the strategy will be wrong). Of course, this analysis may be carried out at different levels, e.g. by product/segment, line of products or entire product portfolio.

QFD analysis is complex, but it may be simplified creating a WHAT versus HOW matrix as illustrated in the table below.

The table helps you to see if your product or service has a sustainable competitive advantage. The first step is to prioritize the WHATs (what customers need). Since companies have limited resources and cannot satisfy all customer needs, it is important to assign importance (priority) to customer requirements.

For example, consider a generic software product such as a payment system. Here is 'WHAT' (customers need): Security is identified as the first customer priority, followed by Fast (the service needs to be delivered quickly), followed by Responsive (it must be always available and work with no errors) and finally, Compatible (it must work on most platforms and systems).

Then align the HOWs against the WHATs, by assessing three questions:

1. Does our HOW fit with the WHAT?
Yes (Y) or No (N).
The features of our product match (Y) or do not match (N) with customers' requirements.

2. Do competitors offer a similar capacity?
Can competitors also deliver their own HOWs (products/service features) that match the WHAT? If 'No'

then you are the only one and therefore insert 'W' in the table below (good news!). If YES, we name the competitor (in the table).

3. Is our position sustainable (medium-long term)?
'Yes' means that our HOW satisfies the customer's WHAT (now and in the medium to longer term) and that position is likely to be maintained somehow (technology, patents, exclusive distribution channels). 'No' means competitors are going to take you over soon (for example by just copying your offering).

QFD matrix example for a software product

HOW

		Fire-wall	Availability	Stan-dards
WHAT:	Imp or-tance			
Secure	1	YWY		
Fast	2		YCompetitor N	
Responsive	3			YWN
Compatible	4			NNN

Assessing 'Secure': YWY
YWY means we deliver 'WHAT' a customer requires: 'Security' by offering a product feature ('HOW'): Firewall. We are the only company offering this 'Secure' feature which is the most important feature required by our customers. We therefore score it 'Y'. Competitors don't have adequate firewalls yet (W) and we can maintain the advantage for a while (Y). YWY is the perfect score.

Assessing 'Fast': YCompetitorN
We have a solution based for example on a proprietary algorithm to authentify users (Y), but some competitors

(Competitor) also have their own algorithms so it doesn't represent a true competitive advantage, i.e. there is no real competitive position to sustain (N).

Assessing 'Responsiveness': YWN
Our product fits with customers' requirement for always working (Y). We have a technology (W) that no competitor has yet (W) but since it is based on published standards it will soon be available to competitors so (N).

Assessing 'Compatible': NNN
'Compatible' is a customer requirement (albeit not a top priority). We don't deliver this, hence 'N'. Do competitors offer a similar capacity? No, so 'N'. Is our position sustainable (medium-long term)? Obviously not as we don't offer this as a feature yet so 'N'. Note this is a feature not delivered yet and could represent an opportunity.
Note: 'N Competitor N'
Would mean that we do not satisfy this particular customer requirement ('N'). There are competitors and obviously this is not a sustainable advantage (as we don't have one right now).
Note 'Y Competitor N'
Would mean that we satisfy this particular customer requirement but there are competitors offering it also and our advantage is not sustainable.

The products/services are composed by all the WHATs versus the HOWs. The marketing team must evaluate if the final product is robust enough to be manufactured and marketed.

The table summarizes our competitive positioning at a detailed level and reflects visually the strong and weak points, linking Strategy with Tactics (often a difficult task) where a product or service needs to be totally defined and ready to go to the market. The analysis helps marketers to consider specific features of a product or service and identify areas for improvement (build differentiation or maintain sustainability).

HOW

		Fire-wall	Availability	Stand-ards
WHAT:	Impor-tance			
Secure	1	YWY		
Fast	2		YCompetitor N	
Responsive	3			YWN
Compatible	4			NNN

So what does the table tell you?

The table reveals that our solution has a very small competitive advantage and we rely on one of the four most important features. The product right now, is competitive but it could fail if some changes in the environment occur, e.g. a new security standard. The table also highlights the possibility of creating a compatible platform which would work on a wide set of platforms (Windows, iPhones, Android, Symbian) which would deliver more advantage. The tool effectively helps to analyze the Competitive Advantage in detail and link it to the real features of a product.

Appendix 8: Monitoring Your Ad's Share Of Voice

Online ads – good news, Google AdWords calculates your SOV for you. Google, <u>SOV</u> is "a relative portion of inventory available to a single advertiser within a defined market sector over a specified time period."

Google defines "inventory" as the impression inventory available against your campaign based on your keyword and campaign settings.

Google AdWords Auction Insights Report allows you to compare your average position with competitors, your impression share, and the amount of times you are above them in search results. If you want to see how to go about setting up a competitor benchmarking process, see my Digital Marketing co-author Dave Chaffey (2017) and his <u>Smart Insights</u> knowledge hub.

References

Adams, P. (2014) Design futures 2: personalization and the new product canvas, Inside Intercom.io

Akhtar, O. (2014) Who is winning the Marketing Cloud wars? The Hub, 5 March

Anders, G. (2012) Jeff Bezos's Top 10 Leadership Lessons, Forbes 4 April.

Band, W. & Hagen, P. (2011) The Right Customer Experience Strategy, Destination CRM, May 2011

Barry, C., Markey, R., Almquist, E. and Brahm, C. (2011) Putting social media to work, Bain Brief, 12 Sep

Bear, J. (2013) 2 Minutes on BrightTALK: Marketing so useful people would pay for it, BrightTALK

Belicove, M (2013) Content Marketing Study Suggests Most Content Marketing Doesn't Work, Forbes 10 Sep

Benady, A. (2014) E-cigarette boss Jacob Fuller on comms and the industry's 'biggest mistake' PR Week, 25 June

Bolling, K. & Smith P. 2017 Declining Response Rates And Their Impact, Ipsos MORI

Bosomworth, D. (2014) Why and how marketers must respond to the decline in organic reach, Smart Insights 19 Aug.

Bossidy, L. & Charan, R.C. (2012) Execution: The Discipline of Getting Things Done , Crown Books

Bukhari, J. (2017) Bond Traders Are Betting Sears Will Go Out of Business in 18 months (Forbes Feb 07)

Campaign Monitor (2019) 7 Stats That Will Make You Rethink Mobile Email, Campaign Monitor, July

Castleman, R. (2020) What impact will voice search have on SEO in 2020?, Search Engine Watch

Clement, J. (2020) Percentage of mobile device website traffic worldwide from 1st, quarter 2015 to 4th quarter 2019, Statista, 29 Jan

Chaffey, D. & Ellis Chadwick, F. (2013) Digital Marketing: Strategy, Implementation and Practice, 5th edition, Pearson

Chaffey, D. & Smith, PR (2013) Emarketing Excellence 4th ed., Routledge

Chaffey, D. (2013) Improve your Competitor analysis and benchmarking Chaffey, D. (2013) Google AdWords Changes in 2013 – reviewing the opportunities and potential problems, Smart Insights 9 Aug.

Chaffey, D. (2013) Introducing RACE: a practical framework to improve your digital marketing, Smart Insights 14 Nov.

Chaffey, D. (2018) The Content Optimization Matrix, SmartInsights 16 Apr

Christensen, C. et al (2016) Know Your Customers' "Jobs to Be Done" HBR September.

Cramer, B. (2014) How should you measure your share of voice? Ragan's PR Daily 10 Jan

Dalton (2012) How brands can leverage the power of visual social media, Media Matters, 20 Dec.

daSilva, T. (2014) Why Ignoring User Intent is Costing You Money in AdWords, Unbounce, 5 Sep

Davey, N. (2018) 9 different customer journey maps (and what we can learn from them) My Customer.com 30 July

Desai, N.* Making customer connections bloom, Saas Customer Stories *no date of publication available

Doyle Slayton (2014) 6 Talents of Modern Day Marketers, LinkedIn 13 May

Duhigg, C. (2012) How Companies Learn Your Secrets, New York Times, 16 Feb

Economist (2016) What bots are, 12 April

Eloqua (2013) White Paper: Revenue Performance Management-Re-Engineering the Revenue Cycle

Forrester Consulting (2013) Use Behavioural Marketing To Up The Ante In The Age Of The Customer, Silverpop.

Everthing (2017), New Smart Handbags from Rebecca Minkoff, Everthng 15 Nov.

Fox Rubin, B. (2019) Amazon is going to kill your Dash button, CNet.com August 1

Foy, H. (2014) Have car shows run out of road? FT, 5 May

Gladstone, B. (2014) 'How To Use Twitter Advanced Search Queries for Leads' Social Media Examiner 5 June.

Goldber, C (2013) Marketing on Mobile: Why is this Platform Different? High Tech Communicator, 3 June

Gray, R. (2013) Retail Revolution, The Marketer Mar/Apr Marketing on Mobile: Why is this Platform Different?, High Tech Communicator, 3 June

Gramlich, J. (2019) Young Americans are less trusting of other people – and key institutions – than their elders, Pew Research Cemtre, Fact Tank August 6

Harari, Y. (2017) The future according to Facebook, FT 25 March

Harrington (2017) Survey: People's Trust Has Declined in Business, Media, Government and NGOs, HBR 16 Jan

Hoffman, R. (2017) Masters of Scale podcast episode 1: 'Handcrafted' interview with Airbnb's Brian Chesky.

Hoffman, R. (2017) Masters of Scale podcast episode 8: 'Imperfect is perfect' interview with Mark Zuckerberg, facebook founder & CEO

Hudson, J. (2014) Disrupt or Die, Wired Magazine, Wired Magazine, 2 Oct

Hurynag, A. (2020) Grieving dad of Molly Russell says tech giants must be forced to hand over data, Sky News 17 Jan

Ibrahim, M (2013) Twitter and WPP in global partnership, PR Week 14 June

Jackson, S. (2009) Cult of Analytics, Routledge

Jankowski, S. (2014) The Sectors Where the Internet of Things Really Matters, HBR Global Edition, 22 October

Jordan, J. (2017) Email Client Market Share Trends for 2017 (So Far), Litmus, JULY 17

Kaye, K. (2013) Data Defined: What Is 'Big Data' Anyway? Ad Age, 15 Jan

Kirkpatrick, D. (2013) Email Optimization: A single word change results in a 90% lift in sign-ups Emarketing Experiments Blog, 15 March

Kirkpatrick, M. (2010) Google CEO Schmidt: People Aren't Ready for the Technology Revolution, ReadWrite, 4 Aug.

Kuppler, T. (2014) Inspiring Passion and Purpose, or Happiness as a Business Model, TLNT 22 May

Laney, D. (2014) The Hidden Tax Advantage of Monetizing Your Data, Forbes 27 Mar

Lee, J (2013) Obama digital director praises social media, Yale News, 9 April

Levine, R., Locke, C., Searles, D. & Weinberger, D. (2000) The ClueTrain Manifesto, Perseus Books.

Lobo, J. (2017) 3 options for using Chatbots for ecommerce, Smart Insights, 11 Dec

Mailchimp (date unknown) Content Style Guide, Mailchimp

Marr, B. (2014) Facebook + WhatsApp = The Ultimate Spying Machine? LinkedIn 27 Feb

Marr, B. (2018) The 4th Industrial Revolution Is Here - Are You Ready? Forbes, 13 Aug.

McGovern, G. (2010) The customer is a stranger, Gerry McGovern/New Thinking, 6 June

McGovern, G. (2014) Customer Convenience, Gerry McGovern/New Thinking, 28 Sep

McGovern, G. (2016) Digital Is The Transformation Agent Not the Transformation, Customer experience insights, 16 Jan

McGovern, G. (2017) We Must Measure Customer Time, Customer Experience Insights 20 Nov

McGovern, G. (2019) Use and convenience replace trust and security, GerryMcGovern.com, 3 Feb.

McLellan, L. (2012), By 2017 the CMO will Spend More on IT Than the CIO Gartner Webinars, 3 Jan.

Meinertzhagen, P. (2013) How to Calculate Share of Voice for Organic Search, The YouMoz Blog, 29 Nov

Miller, J. (2013) 5 LinkedIn Company Page Tips to Enhance Your Marketing, Social Media Examiner 23 Oct.

Moore, K. (2017) How To Increase Your Performance By Finding Your Purpose, Forbes, 3 Aug

Muellner, M. (2013) Three 'Light Bulb Moments' to illuminate social media marketing success, Marketing Profs 31 Oct.

Murphy, J. (2013) Listening vs. Hearing: How to increase your Twitter engagement rate. Bloom Worldwide, 29 July

Novo, J. WebTrends, Take 10 Series Increase Customer Retention by Analyzing Visitor Segments,

O'Connell, M. (2017) Your Animal life is Over. Your Machine Life Has Begun. The road to immortality, The Guardian, 25 Mar.

Olsen, L. (2017) Rebecca Minkoff Releases Line of 'Smart' Bags, WWD Nov 10.

Paget, J. (2013) 'Searching For The Real Value Of Facebook Marketing, Smart Insights Oct 24

Perrin, A. (2017) New Smart Handbags From Rebecca Minkoff, Blogthng Nov 15

Porter, E. & Hepplemann, J. (2014), How Smart, Connected Products Are Transforming Competition, Harvard Business Review, Nov.

Pulizzi, J. (2013) Measuring the Impact of Your Content Marketing Strategy: The Pyramid Approach, The Content Marketing Institute, 1 June

Radcliff, C. (2014) Why you should be monitoring your brand on Twitter, Econsultancy 14 July

Richardson, A. (2010) Reimagining the customer experience, HBR Oct 28

Ritson, M. (2017) Why Social Media Is Mostly A Waste Of Time for Marketers, Melbourne Business School

Roach, J. (2014) The 10-Point Social Media Policy Everyone Will Understand, Sociallogical, 2 June

Rogers, B. (2013) Seeking CMOs: Must Know Big Data and Digital Marketing, Forbes 15 Jan

Sandel, M. (2017) ' Why The Democrats are so out of touch with the People', World Economic Forum, Davos 2017 – (a very interesting video).

Satell, G. (2014) Are We Ready For The Personal Web? Forbes 25 Jan

Satell, G. (2012) 4 Essential Questions to Ask About Your Digital Strategy, Digital Tonto, 17 Oct

Schaefer, M (2014) Content Shock: Why content marketing is not a sustainable strategy, BusinessesGrow.com, 6 Jan

Schaefer, M. (2019) Marketing Rebellion, Mark Schaefer Solutions, BusinessesGrow.com

Schwab, K. (2018) The Fourth Industrial Revolution, World Economic Forum

Seybold P. (2001) Get Inside the Lives of your customers, HBR May

Silverpop, (2013) New Study: Despite Benefits, Most Marketers Still Not Capitalizing on Behaviours, Silverpop, 10 July

Simply Measured, (2014) How To Use Facebook Data To Analyze Your Competitors

Sisario, B (2014) Venture Will Mine Twitter for Music's Next Big Thing, New York Times, 2 Feb.

Sisodia, R., Sheth, J. and Wolfe, D. (2014) Firms of Endearment: How World–Class Companies Profit from Passion and Purpose, 2nd ed., Pearson Education

Smart Insights: 'Digital Marketing Capability Analysis' & other free benchmarking templates SmartInsights.com

Smith , PR (2018) How Rats Work = How Twitter Works? prsmith.org/blog 25 Sep.

Smith, PR (2014) 'How Integrated Content Marketing Creates Competitive Advantage, prsmith.org/blog 6 Nov

Smith, PR (2014) The Rise and Fall Of Owned and Earned But Not Paid Media – World Cup Marketing Wars? prsmith.org/blog 27 June

Smith, PR (2011) SOSTAC® Guide To Writing The Perfect Plan, prsmith.org/sostac

Smith, PR and Zook, Z. (2012) Marketing Communications – integrating offline and online with social, Kogan Page

Smith, PR (2013) Gamification The Good,The Bad and The Ugly, PR Smith Marketing Blog 22 Aug.

Smith, PR (2014) Research Driven Shock Ad Uses Magic Formula and Goes Viral PR Smith Marketing Blog, 23 Aug

Smith, PR (2013) PR Smith Marketing Blog prsmith.org/blog

PR Smith (2016) The IoT Is Here, PR Smith Blog, prsmith.org/blog 13 Jan

Smith, PR (2017) How Trump Won (a SOSTAC® Analysis) – Part 1, PR Smith Marketing Blog prsmith.org/blog 20 Jan

Smith, PR (2017) How Trump Won (a SOSTAC® Analysis) – Part 2, PR Smith Marketing Blog prsmith.org/blog 20 Jan

Smith, PR & Zook, Z. (2020) Marketing Communications – integrating online and offline, customer engagement and digital technologies, 7th ed. Kogan Page

Smith, PR (2019) Imagine You Could Do This With Video PRsmith.org/blog Apr 18,

Solis, B. (2012) There's too much talking in social media and not enough listening and learning. TEDTalk: Reinventing Consumer Capitalism – Screw Business as Usual

Soumya, P. (2017) The Story of Amazon.com- Jeff Bezos, Innovation, Customer Centricity, Linkedin Pulse 24 July

Space Between (date not published), Fashion eCommerce Retail UX & CRO Report, Space Between

Spool, J. (2009) The $300 Million Button, User Interface Engineering, 14 Jan

Stryker, C. (2014) Big Data will impact every part of your life, TEDxFultonStreet 22 Sep

Sullivan, C (2014) 17 ways to F**k-up your AB Testing, Smart Insights 16 Sep

Takahashi, D. (2013) IBM researcher can decipher your personality from looking at 200 of your tweets, VB Science, 8 Oct

ThisIsMoney.com (2020) Apple sold more watches than the entire Swiss watch industry last year, Daily Mail City & Finance 07 Feb

Toll, E. (2014) Content Marketing Strategy – 5 Essential Tips , Champion Communications 18 Sep

Toner, L. (2014) 6 Ways Social Data Can Inform Your Marketing Strategy, Hubspot, Inbound Marketing

Urbany, J., & Davis, J. (2007). Strategic Insight in Three Circles. Retrieved January 2010, Harvard Business Review, The Magazine, November.

Urbany, J. E, & Davis, J. H. (2010). Grow by Focusing on What Matters: Strategy in 3-Circles. Vermont, USA: Business Expert Press.

Woods, S. (2009) Digital Body Language – deciphering customer intentions in an online world, New Year Publishing.

Weintraub, M (2013) The Definitive Share Of Voice Guide: PPC, SEO, Social and Multi-Channel SOV Models, AmIClearBlog Sep 6   .

Young, Y. (2014) Urban Myths and Their Disastrous Effects on Marketing, Cambridge Marketing College

A Final Word re the layout of your plan

Feel free to lay out your plan in whatever format you or your organization prefers. For example, it's quite common to have an executive summary at the very start. Some organizations state big objectives (mission and vision statements) at the beginning and sometimes they also include major financial goals.

Others prefer to see large chunks of the detailed Situation Analysis dumped into the appendices at the end of the document. Realistically, senior management initially just want to see your targets (objectives) and a summary of how you will achieve them (strategy).

Either way, half of your plan should be devoted to the Situation Analysis. Regardless of the final structure, if you address each section of SOSTAC® + 3Ms, under whatever name or headings you prefer, you will have covered all the key ingredients for a great plan.

Good luck with it.
Paul Smith

PS Feedback Is Welcome
Please do let me know what you think of this book. All feedback and suggestions are most welcome and appreciated. Please use the dedicated feedback section on my website prsmith.org/feedback page.

PPS For more on SOSTAC® Certified Planners & SOSTAC® Certified Companies go to www.SOSTAC.org

Keep In Touch

PRSmith.org

PR Smith Marketing

@PR_Smith

PR Smith Marketing

PR Smith Marketing

PRPSmith

GreatSportsmanship.org

Great Sportsmanship

@GtSportsmanship

GreatSportsmanshipProgramme

GreatSportsmanshipProgramme

great.sportsmanship

For more on SOSTAC® workshops and webinars and certified SOSTAC® planners, consultants and trainers visit: prsmith.org/sostac.

Your Next 3 Steps

1. Become a SOSTAC® Certified Planner
Download the manuals, watch a short video, see some mini case studies. Take the online, open book, multiple choice mini-case. Approved by UK's CPD Standards Office.

2. Adopt SOSTAC® Planning in your organisation
Write better plans. Boost effectiveness. Share a common structure. Boost efficiency. Workbooks and templates accelerate the adoption of SOSTAC® Planning.

3. Enjoy a SOSTAC® Planning workshop or talk
Inspire your organisation with a workshop or talk at your next conference or seminar. Please contact me through any of the channels listed in the footer.

Don't Forget:

Tell Us Your SOSTAC® Story

Tell us how SOSTAC® helped you. Or just tell us of any innovative, creative or highly effective marketing. We'll polish it and possibly publish it (with your permission) in the next edition of this book or one of Paul's other books.

Write a short Review

If you like this book, please do write a short review on amazon. Or please send any other feedback to me via prsmith.org/feedback.

Visit www.SOSTAC.org

and **become a SOSTAC® Certified Planner**

Equipped with this book, you have the knowledge to take the assessment and become a SOSTAC® Certified Planner.

Printed in Great Britain
by Amazon